THE GREAT COMIC BOOK ARTISTS

THE GREAT COMIC BOOK ARTISTS

RON GOULART

ST. MARTIN'S PRESS · NEW YORK

Editor: Stuart Moore

Production Editors: Victor Guerra, Amit Shah

Design by Paolo Pepe

Library of Congress Cataloging in Publication Data

Goulart, Ron, 1933–
    The great comic book artists.

    1. Comic books, strips, etc.—United States—
History and criticism. 2. Comic books, strips, etc.—
United States—Bibliography. 3. Cartoonists—United
States—Bibliography. I. Title.
PN6725.G63   1986   741.5'092'2 [B]   86-3711
ISBN 0-312-34557-7 (pbk.)

10 9 8 7 6 5 4 3 2

Acknowledgments

*A tip of the slouch hat to Jerry Bails, Mike Barson,
Jerry DeFuccio, Don and Maggie Thompson, Bruce
Hamilton of Another Rainbow, Russ Cochran, and Steve
Saffel of Marvel Comics. All of them are
Great Comic Book Mavens.*

Contents

Introduction	1	Harvey Kurtzman	62
		Joe Maneely	64
Neal Adams	2	Jesse Marsh	66
Matt Baker	4	Sheldon Mayer	68
Carl Barks	6	Mort Meskin	70
Dan Barry	8	Frank Miller	72
C. C. Beck	10	Bob Montana	74
Charles Biro	12	Klaus Nordling	76
Dick Briefer	14	George Pérez	78
John Buscema	16	Wendy Pini	80
John Byrne	18	Bob Powell	82
George Carlson	20	Mac Raboy	84
Howard Chaykin	22	Jerry Robinson	86
Gene Colan	24	John Romita, Sr.	88
Jack Cole	26	Alex Schomburg	90
Reed Crandall	28	John Severin	92
Jack Davis	30	Joe Shuster	94
Steve Ditko	32	Bill Sienkewicz	96
Will Eisner	34	Walt Simonson	98
Lee Elias	36	John Stanley	100
George Evans	38	James Steranko	102
Bill Everett	40	Frank Thorne	104
Lou Fine	42	Alex Toth	106
Frank Frazetta	44	George Tuska	108
Fred Guardineer	46	Ed Wheelan	110
Paul Gustavson	48	Al Williamson	112
Bob Kane	50	Barry Windsor-Smith	114
Gil Kane	52	Basil Wolverton	116
Walt Kelly	54	Wally Wood	118
Jack Kirby	56	Berni Wrightson	120
Bernard Krigstein	58		
Joe Kubert	60	Bibliography	123

THE GREAT COMIC BOOK ARTISTS

Introduction

Up until 1935 only a handful of people in America would have been able to list their occupation as comic book artist. There were Vic Pazmino, doing filler pages for the pioneering *Famous Funnies;* Norman Marsh, who'd turned out one issue of *Detective Dan* in 1933; and Boody Rogers and Tack Knight, who'd contributed to the ill-fated *The Funnies* back in 1929 and 1930. A dapper ex-cavalry officer named Malcolm Wheeler-Nicholson changed that when, with considerable enthusiasm and not much cash, he launched *New Fun* early in 1935. He followed it toward the end of that year with *New* and from then on there was an original material comic book industry, albeit a shaky one. The major recruited to his staff struggling art school students, down-on-their-luck pulp magazine illustrators, alcoholic newspaper cartoonists, and others who hoped to earn a few bucks in that grim Depression year.

The history of the rise and growth of the comic book is not our subject. Suffice it to say that in the years since Major Nicholson set up shop down on Fourth Avenue in Manhattan, the field has grown considerably and that hundreds of men and a few dozen women have worked as comic book artists. Today you can even buy books on how to be one or take a college course on the subject.

The Great Comic Book Artists is about three score of the best practitioners of graphic story art. Artists from every decade since the thirties are to be found here, along with biographical material and samples of their work. At the end of the book you'll find a bibliography with suggestions on how to collect their work—economically, whenever possible.

Keep in mind that "great" is a tricky word and that one person's great may well be another's lousy. Also, there were a few great comic book artists who couldn't draw very well. For details on this seeming paradox, consult the biographies that follow. I've tried to produce a balanced book, but I must admit I slipped in a few highly subjective choices.

If you don't find one or two of your own favorites here, remember that we could only fit sixty candidates into this present volume. Be patient and it's possible you'll eventually see *The Great Comic Book Artists II.* Until then. . .

—Ron Goulart

Neal Adams

It was in the late 1960s that Adams began to shake up the comic book field. Going to work for DC after five years as the artist on the *Ben Casey* newspaper strip, he was soon impressing comic book readers and editors alike with his innovative layouts and grandstanding drawing style. *Ben Casey,* based on the popular TV hospital melodrama, had begun in 1962. Although he was only twenty-one at the time, Adams felt confident. "It was a very popular strip and sold as well as any other realistic strip at the time and better than most," he's said. "The reason for that was that I added things to it that went above and beyond the soap opera aspect of it. . . . One of the things I added was that I told a story every day, in three panels."

What Adams brought to funnybooks, just as they were moving into a more realistic and socially aware phase, was the slick realism of newspaper story strips and advertising art. He had a sophisticated, bravura style, somewhat reminiscent of the sort of thing Stan Drake and Lou Fine were doing at the time. When it came to laying out a story, though, Adams was much more unconventional than the competition. His panels sliced pages up in unexpected ways, his long and medium shots favored unusual angles and perspectives, and his close-ups rarely showed his heroes striking a handsome pose. The work was both slick and gritty, sort of soap opera with warts. Of the impact he had, Adams says, "It was strange because nobody at that time expected somebody to show up with so many new ideas or what seemed like new ideas. I took everybody by surprise. . . . My entrance into the field caused a lot of uproar and mixed up even more a bowl that had already been mixed by Jack Kirby and other people, and just caused it to go crazier."

Adams first attracted attention with the Deadman character, which he started drawing in DC's *Strange Adventures* in 1967. This red-clad, white-hued hero earned his name the hard way, by being murdered while performing his circus trapeze act. Despite the impressive artwork, Deadman was not a hit and he left the magazine in 1969. Next Adams worked on the Spectre, DC's original deadman superhero. After that he took a turn with Batman. "He brought back something sadly lacking in Batman's character," says *Comics Journal,* "that sense of the mysterious, the eerie, the supernatural which was originally an integral part of the caped crusader's mystique. . . . Visually, the Batman's cape lengthened, draping over the crimebuster's shoulders like Dracula's cloak. His face and mask were continually submerged in shadow. . . . Even today, the character is still often depicted in the Adams style."

Teaming up with writer Denny O'Neil, Adams then guided long-time hero Green Lantern through the "relevance" period of his career. The Green Lantern, working with the Green Arrow—who was updated to look somewhat like an aging, and well-groomed, hippy—tackled social problems such as pollution, overpopulation, women's rights, racial prejudice, drugs, and political corruption. Adams, something of a social crusader himself, was obviously inspired by this sort of material and put a good deal of work into the stories. Despite the good intentions of DC and the handsome packaging of the messages, the *Green Lantern* title failed to succeed and was cancelled in the spring of 1972. Writing of this period in GL's career, O'Neil quotes editor Julius Schwartz as saying that it was "a success *and* a failure. Personally, yes, a great success. Plenty of publicity, no extra sales." When the magazine was revived in 1976, it was studiously irrelevant.

Adams has moved in and out of comics ever since, alternating with advertising and illustration work. He's drawn for Marvel, DC, and the alternate publishers. In 1982, for instance, he began *Ms. Mystic* for Pacific Comics—"An ecological superheroine. I think there are more problems on Earth than bank robbers, and if you want to deal with an Earth that bears some semblance to reality, you must recognize the problems of today. One of the problems is that we're screwing up our planet. This is a character who, in an exaggerated form, fights for Earth." Her career, like that of other of the restless Adams's creations, has been erratic. Among his other recent comic book projects are *Echo of Futurepast* and *Zero Patrol.*

He doesn't see himself as simply an illustrator or an artist. "I think of myself," he says, "as a storyteller who uses drawing."

The X-Men in a dramatic moment, courtesy Neal Adams. Script by Roy Thomas, inks by Tom Palmer. (Copyright © 1969 Marvel Comics Group.)

Matt Baker

Baker was not an artist of wide-ranging abilities. What he drew best was pretty women. He was, in fact, one of the leading practitioners of what's come to be called "Good Girl Art." In the years he spent in comics he drew every sort of attractive female from Phantom Lady to Lorna Doone. Much admired and much imitated, he was sort of the Vargas of comic books.

One of the few blacks to work in the field, Baker started his career at the Iger shop in 1944. He was in his early twenties and Iger describes him as being "handsome and nattily dressed." According to Iger, Baker's "only sample was a color sketch of (naturally) a beautiful gal! On the strength of that, and a nod from my associate editor Ruth Roche, he was hired as a background artist. It didn't take long for Mr. Baker to develop. . . . His drawing was superb. His women were gorgeous!"

Baker had come along as comics were moving into new areas. Stimulated by impressive wartime sales to an audience that had been swollen by the addition of thousands and thousands of GIs—older and raunchier than earlier readers—many publishers beefed up their product. Those old standbys, sex and violence, proliferated. In the years immediately after World War II, true crime and horror comics, all decorated with sexy women, continued to flourish. Superheroes floundered in those years. An artist who could draw pretty women as well as Baker was in demand, so much so that, according to some who knew him, he overworked himself. He was not yet forty when he died.

The major purveyors of Good Girl Art in the forties were Fiction House and Fox. Baker's pages, rich with his patented brand of slim, large-breasted and long-legged heroine, appeared frequently in titles of both companies. He was especially good with jungle girls who went in for skimpy animal-skin outfits—Tiger Girl in *Fight Comics,* Camilla in *Jungle,* etc. It was for Victor Fox's somewhat sleazy company that Baker drew his most famous character, Phantom Lady. She'd first appeared, looking rela-

tively sedate, in the fall of 1941 in the pages of *Police Comics.* In 1947 Fox got his hands on the character and she began appearing in a magazine of her own. The move changed her somewhat. Her costume became even skimpier and her bosom grew impressively larger. She also developed a marked fondness for being tied up and chained, especially on covers.

Although the Phantom Lady lasted less than two years in her Fox incarnation, she made a lasting impression. Baker's boyishly enthusiastic pinup artwork is one of the reasons, as are the elements pointed out in *The Comic Book Price Guide*—"negligee cover," "classic bondage cover," etc. Dr. Frederic Wertham was impressed, too, though not favorably. In his 1954 study of the negative effects of comics, *Seduction of the Innocent,* he reprinted Baker's cover from *Phantom Lady* #17 and captioned it, "Sexual stimulation by combining 'headlights' with the sadist's dream of tying up a woman." The doctor's comment has had the unintended effect of making this the most expensive issue of the eleven Baker was associated with. It's worth as much as $850 today.

Since Iger's shop provided art for the Gilberton company, Baker even got to draw an issue of *Classics Illustrated.* He didn't get completely away from pretty girls, since the novel he adapted was *Lorna Doone.* That appeared as #32 (December, 1946) and showed that Baker could draw other things than sexy girls.

As the pressures on comics to clean up their act increased, Baker had fewer opportunities to practice his specialty. He drew Westerns, war stories, true crime, and romance in the early 1950s, tried his hand at *Lassie* in the middle 1950s, and did more Westerns in the late 1950s, this time for Marvel. There has been some disagreement as to when Baker died, the most common date given being 1956. Recently, however, Vince Colleta, in whose studio he was working at the time of his death, has stated that the year was 1962. He also added that Baker was "one of the snappiest dressers I ever knew."

Good Girl Art at its best in this Tiger Girl page. Although a pinup, she spoke in an impressive Shakespearean manner. *(Copyright © 1948 Fiction House, Inc.)*

Carl Barks

The Great Unknown during his active years in comics, Barks remained uncredited and vitually unheralded until after he retired. Known only as "the Good Artist," or some variation thereof, to most fans, he worked at turning out his inimitable *Donald Duck* stories from 1942 into the 1960s. He was a one-man band, writing, pencilling, and inking. In the years since he quit being the chronicler of life in Duckburg he has become increasingly well-known. Today Barks is internationally acknowledged as one of the handful of geniuses produced by comic books during their first half-century. "A genius of the first rank," *Nemo* magazine has called him, "wholly American in his self-effacing production."

Barks was born in the wilds of eastern Oregon in 1901. "How I came to be a cartoonist is as much a mystery to me as it would be to anybody else," he's admitted. "I have no cartoonists in my ancestral tree whatsoever, no artists that I know of, no writers that I know of." But "by the time I was sixteen, I had become pretty well assured that I wanted to be an artist or a cartoonist." Before attaining his goal, however, "I had to go out and be a cowhand and a farmer, a muleskinner, lumberjack, anything that happened to come along that would furnish me with a living. I'd worked in a printing shop, been a cowboy and a whole bunch of other things, with practically no success whatever."

Not until the late 1920s did he begin to sell his cartoons—"I didn't try *The New Yorker* or the ones who were paying high prices because every cartoonist that free-lanced at all was already crowding that market." Aiming a mite lower, Barks hit *Judge* and *College Humor.* He was even more successful with markets that went in for what then would have been labeled risqué material. His gags, built around well-built ladies in varying states of undress, found favor with a publication called *The Calgary Eye-Opener.* In 1931 the Minneapolis-based magazine offered him a staff job—"just sort of a handy gag man around the office"—at the handsome salary of $110 a month. By 1935 "the wages were getting smaller by the hour," and Barks decided to apply for a job with the Walt Disney studios out in California. His samples prompted an offer to try out, at $20 per week, as an in-betweener in the Southern California animation works. "I went out there on a wild gamble that I could make it."

He made it, but not exactly as an artist. "I don't think I would ever have finished the period of training before I got fired," he's said, "but I turned in so many gags to the comic strip department and the story department . . . that I got put in the story department on a permanent basis." After serving nearly seven years there Barks decided to leave Disney and settle in the desert country. "I was thinking that if I could get out there to this ranch and raise chickens to make money, in my spare time I could develop a character of my own—a sort of Superman or one of those things. I'd thought of doing something with human types of characters and I wanted to see if I could develop something along that line." It was ducks, not chickens, that were to fill the next twenty-five years of Barks' life.

Before leaving Disney he'd worked on a one-shot comic book titled *Donald Duck Finds Pirate Gold.* Based on an abandoned movie, this was the first original Donald Duck comic book ever done. "I did part of the drawing only," explains Barks about the 1942 magazine. "The other pages were by Jack Hannah. Bob Karp did the script." Late in 1942 Barks learned that Dell-Western was looking for people to do original ten-page stories to add to *Walt Disney's Comics & Stories.* He got the job and his first work appeared in #31 (April, 1943). Fairly soon he was writing as well as drawing the adventures. The character of Donald changed as Barks began to think of him as his own. "Instead of making just a quarrelsome little guy out of him, I made a sympathetic character. He was sometimes a villain, and he was often a real good guy and at all times he was just a blundering person like the average human being." The three diminutive nephews changed, too. "I broadened them like I did Donald, started out with mischievous little guys and ended up with little scientists, you might say."

Barks took on full-length Donald books in 1943 as well. It was in these—*The Mummy's Ring, Frozen Gold, Volcano Valley,* etc.—that he really came into his own. With room to swing, he began creating graphic novels full of adventure, comedy, satire, and some of the best cartooning to be found in comics. Nineteen forty-seven saw the publication of *Christmas on Bear Mountain* and the introduction of Barks's major creation, Uncle Scrooge.

Barks retired at the age of sixty-five and devoted himself to painting. He left Donald and the nephews, along with his own Scrooge, Gyro Gearloose, Gladstone Gander, and the villainous Beagle Boys to other, less gifted, hands. His work has been continuously reprinted since then. Even his own publishers eventually got around to acknowledging him—after fans from just about everywhere had been writing about and extolling him for years—and in some 1974 trade paperback reprints they mentioned him by name in the introductions, pointing out that his work is "cherished by comic book fans throughout the world."

Ducks, Beagle Boys, and a nice demonstration of Barks' skills. *(Copyright © 1986 The Walt Disney Company.)*

Dan Barry

One of the dominant styles of the decade following the Second World War was that of Dan Barry. He flourished in the years during which comic books were expanding into new categories—realistic adventure, true crime, romance, Western, sophisticated fantasy. Although he did excellent work on superheroes and cowboys, his major strength was in drawing plainclothes heroes. His style blended the figure work of Alex Raymond and the lush inking and realistic backgrounds of Milton Caniff with considerable input of his own. Barry brought a slickness to comic books that would have been out of place a few years earlier.

Born in New Jersey in 1923, he began in comics while in his late teens. He was a protégé of artist-novelist George Mandel and teamed up with George's brother Alan Mandel on some of his earliest jobs—usually using the joint pen name Emby. When, after three years in the air force, he returned to comic books in 1946, his style had matured considerably.

For Hillman's *Airboy* he drew the title character, ably rendering both the aircraft and the pretty women required, and that walking compost pile and precursor of Swamp Thing, the Heap. At Fawcett Barry took a turn with Commando Yank in *Wow Comics.* He also turned out quite a few adventure yarns, ranging from pirate tales to stories of mountain climbing in Tibet, for the comic magazines that were given away in the Buster Brown shoe stores.

For the Lev Gleason titles Barry worked on both costumed heroes—the original Daredevil and Crimebuster—and on gangster stuff for *Crime Does Not Pay.* At this point, in the late 1940s, editor-writer Charles Biro was moving Daredevil and Crimebuster away from derring-do and into social problem areas—juvenile delinquency, etc.—and Barry's developing style, with its well-documented realism, was well suited to the new direction.

His most impressive work in the costumed hero department was done for DC at about the same time. For *Adventure* he drew Johnny Quick, the roadshow Flash, and for *Action* he took over Vigilante, the cowboy crimebuster. This latter feature was sometimes urban and sometimes rural and Barry did it all well, drawing motorcycles and mustangs with equal ease. He had, by now, also developed a distinctive style of pretty girl.

Gang Busters, the true-crime radio show whose machine-guns-and-sirens opening gave the phrase "Coming on like Gang Busters" to the language, first took to the air in the middle 1930s; it remained on until the late 1950s and was adapted to several other media. In 1947 DC took over the comic book version and Barry was the star of the early issues, drawing covers and the opening story. Since DC's approach to crime was never as violent or explicit as that of Gleason and many of their other competitors, Barry's work in *Gang Busters* is a bit more sedate than it was elsewhere. As DC continued to branch out, Barry took on new chores. He drew the first issue of *Alan Ladd* and the early issues of *Big Town,* another radio crime show adaptation.

It was in the postwar years that several comic book artists graduated to newspaper strips—Mac Raboy, John Lehti, Paul Norris, etc. Barry drew his first syndicated strip in 1948, when he was given the *Tarzan* daily. This was not an especially lucrative assignment and he stayed with it less than a year, improving the apeman's looks appreciably before he departed. The *Flash Gordon* daily was revived in 1951 and Barry got the job, one he's kept, more or less, ever since. This was not Raymond's light opera Flash, but a hero with whom reality had to some extent caught up. While the emphasis was on adventure, the continuities were like the sort of thing being done in the latest science fiction stories and novels. Barry's most impressive work was done on the initial years of *Flash Gordon;* a growing interest in painting caused him eventually to farm out much of the work on the strip. Today he shares the credit on the daily and Sunday with Bob Fujitani, another comic book vet, and his hand is no longer evident.

WITH A STROKE OF LUCK, THE HEAP PLUNGES HIS CLAW INTO THE SOFT FLESH BETWEEN THE DEVILFISH'S EYES - HIS ONE WEAK SPOT! LIMP WITH PAIN, THE OCTOPUS DESCENDS BELOW THE SURFACE AGAIN...

... PURSUING HIS ADVANTAGE, THE HEAP BITES DEEP INTO THE WOUND, DRAWING THE BLOOD OF THE SEA-DEMON... AN INKY SUBSTANCE BLURS THE WATER... AND THEN A RED FLOW... THE SIGN OF THE BATTLE'S END....

... AND THE HEAP EMERGES... SUCKING IN THE GOOD CLEAN AIR OF LIFE... THE PRIZE OF THE VICTOR!

THE HEAP HAS BROKEN THE EVIL SPELL OVER OUR FORBIDDEN POOL! NOW THE PEARLS CAN BE RESTORED TO THE ALTAR OF PEACE!

THE GODS HAVE SMILED ON US!

LET US SEE THAT THE HEAP IS NEVER IN WANT OF FOOD AND WATER! HE WILL NOT NEED TO DESTROY OUR LANDS TO BE FED!

AGAIN, O'HEAP, YOU HAVE SHOWN MAN THAT HIS FEAR OF YOU COMES FROM WITHIN THE WARPED CAVERNS OF HIS OWN MIND! YOU HAVE SURVIVED THE JUNGLE - AND *NOW* YOU MUST GO ON TO MEET THE CHALLENGE OF OTHER PLACES!

THE END.

Here Barry applies his abilities to that affable monster, the Heap. *(Copyright © 1948 Hillman Periodicals, Inc.)*

C. C. Beck

A dedicated curmudgeon who once claimed to be the model for the extravagantly nasty Sivana, Charles Clarence Beck didn't enter the comic book field until he was almost thirty. That was late in 1939, when he and editor-writer Bill Parker created the original Captain Marvel. For good measure Parker invented all the other characters for *Whiz Comics,* and Beck drew two more of them —Ibis and Spy Smasher.

Born in Minnesota in 1910, Beck studied art at the Chicago Academy of Fine Art. After a varied career, which included advertising art and painting comic characters like Smitty and Little Orphan Annie on lamp shades, he went to work for Fawcett Publications. That was in 1934, when the publishers were still based in Minnesota. Beck provided cartoons for several humor magazines, including *Smokehouse Monthly* and *Captain Billy's Whiz Bang.* "One guy would work in charcoal, another guy'd do multiline in full color," he has recalled. "My job was imitating all those styles." Fawcett eventually moved to New York City and in 1939 decided to enter the comic book business. Beck was the man the higher-ups picked to try his hand at drawing a competitor for the now impressively thriving Superman. The result was Captain Marvel. Realizing that a fairly close approximation of the Man of Steel, in appearance at any rate, was what was wanted, "we proceeded to give them a character that *looked* somewhat like Superman, but in character was entirely different, and of course none of the big shots ever read it, so they were happy in their ignorance. They put it out and the public grabbed it right away, because it was different. And it was good."

Beck, who has often expressed a lack of enthusiasm for the entire comic book industry, has the distinction of having drawn the most successful superhero of the 1940s. He maintains, however, that Captain Marvel outsold Superman, Batman, and the rest not because of his artwork but because of superior scripts. "It was the story," he's said, "and my belief is that readers only looked at the pictures out of the corners of their eyes." Be that as it may, Beck devoted considerable thought to how to best illustrate the adventures of the Big Red Cheese. "The basis I go on is never put in a single line that isn't necessary. Don't try to show off," he's explained, adding, "You don't throw in anything. You cut your backgrounds down to symbols."

Beck's style was a blend of the illustrative and the cartoony, with attention paid to simplicity, clarity, and design—an individual version of the approach to be seen in the work of such Chicago-based cartoonists as Chester Gould and Harold Gray. "To make comics read properly," Beck feels, "you have to arrange your speech to read from left panel to right panel, and you have to put your characters in those positions. You don't suddenly have a view from the bottom of a well or through a keyhole, looking at their toes or something. And it always seemed to me more or less like a Punch and Judy show, with the two little characters facing each other and not the audience."

Beck's work can be seen at its best in the first two dozen issues of *Whiz Comics,* in material done before the increasingly popularity of Captain Marvel required more material than one man could produce. In these eleven- and twelve-page adventures of the World's Mightiest Mortal, Beck demonstrates his theories on how to tell a graphic story as Billy Batson and his burly alter ego tangle with the snide and diminutive Sivana (one of the most appealing mad scientists in comics), his lovely blonde daughter Beautia, and assorted other crooks, madmen, and monsters. Beck's style was ideally suited to the fantastic, and not quite serious, exploits of Captain Marvel. On some of the earlier escapades the assistance of Pete Costanza, his long-time partner, is in evidence. But a good deal of the stuff is pure, uncluttered Beck.

He was also responsible for the first complete Captain Marvel book, *Special Edition Comics* (1940). Fawcett farmed out the first issues of *Captain Marvel Adventures* to Jack Kirby, George Tuska, and others. Beck eventually had a hand in the title, but his major contribution was the covers. He also drew a majority of the *Whiz* covers, exhibiting a strong poster sense. One of the reasons for the significant sales of Captain Marvel titles was certainly the effective packaging Beck provided.

He stayed with his creation until Fawcett shut down comic operations in 1953. When the character was revived by DC twenty years later, Beck was persuaded to return. He contributed to ten issues before a falling-out occurred. He didn't like the scripts. "The original stories were exciting, varied, professionally handled. DC's were dull, boring, and childish." He's done no comic book work since and, as a result of a recent stroke, does very little drawing at all. He lives, as he has for many years, in Florida, and sums up his career by saying, "I'm really just a commercial illustrator and always have been."

A nicely designed page, featuring both "that big lump of muscle" and his favorite foe.

He was not exactly a great artist, at least not in a strict academic sense. But what he lacked in technical skills Biro made up for in inventiveness and audacity. A terrific packager of his material, he devised numerous ways to hook the reader. He possessed, in addition to a pretty good knack for storytelling, the skills of an advertising agency art director and a carnival barker. Starting out as a humorous cartoonist in the middle 1930s, he switched to superheroes in the wake of Superman and then moved on to a brutal sort of realism. An important figure in the history of comic books—*The World Encyclopedia of Comics* calls him, somewhat extravagantly, "the finest editor and writer" of the 1940s—Biro cooked up formats and techniques that influenced the entire industry and are still in evidence.

Biro was born in 1911, in New York, which made him a few years older than most of the young artists and writers who entered the comic book field in the thirties. In 1936 he went to work for the enterprising Harry "A" Chesler, who owned the very first sweat shop devoted to producing art and editorial material for comic books. Even though there weren't many comic books being published in those lean early years, Chesler managed to thrive and Biro soon became the supervisor of the operation, guiding the likes of Jack Cole, Gill Fox, Ken Ernst, Carl Burgos, and Jack Binder. After leaving Chesler, Biro moved over to MLJ and ran things on *Pep Comics, Top-Notch,* and the rest of that house's pre-Archie titles. It was while at MLJ that Biro, as artist, writer, and editor, abandoned his interest in cute "bigfoot" cartooning. What he developed next was a blend of action, violence, bloodshed, and slinky sex.

Biro's major creation at MLJ was Steel Sterling, which began in *Zip Comics* #1 (February, 1940). Biro's anatomy was shaky, as was his grasp of perspective, but he had a strong sense of action. His early pages, though often crudely drawn, have movement and life. When he began working for the Lev Gleason outfit, Biro came into his own. He took over the original Daredevil—created for *Silver Streak Comics* by Jack Binder and improved upon by Jack Cole—and when DD got his own magazine in 1941, Biro was one of its editors. He also drew the character. In his first Daredevil yarn, Biro pitted his crimson-and-blue hero against a sexy lady who was actually a reanimated mummy. Unlike many of his do-gooder contemporaries, DD was not above sharing a glass of wine and a warm embrace with a lovely lady.

Besides exploiting the blend of sex and violence that was an MLJ hallmark, Biro added packaging tricks that became standard for the field. From its first issue *Daredevil* bore the slogan, "The Greatest Name In Com-

ics," and there were boxes of copy and multicolor headlines promising all sorts of delights, including money—$100 CASH PRIZES You May WIN—to be found within. Biro developed the habit early on of addressing his readers directly, often hyping the story that was about to unfold. "None can rival the wild fantasy that will unfold within these pages! . . . So dim the lights and lock your doors well for this monster might strike at even YOU!" He was also great at teasing the customers. A story entitled *The Case of the Mysterious Trunk* was originally announced for #5 but didn't show up until #7. In #5 Biro explained, "Due to a serious event, it is unwise for me to present 'The Case of the Mysterious Trunk' this month as promised."

Biro's next invention was *Boy Comics,* which debuted in the spring of 1942. The idea here was "a boy hero in every strip!!" This new magazine, coedited with Bob Wood, was announced with typical Biro flair. "Ready at last! The million dollar comic magazine! Two years in the making! Produced behind closed doors in utmost secrecy!" The star feature was Crimebuster, drawn by Biro. The lad tangled with some foul villains, especially Iron Jaw, a Nazi agent who had the lower half of his face replaced by metal. Iron Jaw was given to remarks like, "Why can't the FOOLS realize that we are the superior race!! They must and they will . . . if I have to kill every last one of them! I SWEAR IT!!" Biro also stuck compelling blurbs on his *Boy* covers—"First Torture, Then DEATH! With 130,000,000 Lives At Stake! Can CRIMEBUSTER Squelch This Foul Jap Treachery?"

Close on the heels of *Boy* came Biro's prime creation, *Crime Does Not Pay.* While not the first true crime comic book—McKay had published a *Gang Busters* one-shot, based on the radio show, as early as 1938—*Crime Does Not Pay* was the first one to gain impressive sales. The advent of World War II had added an enormous number of comic book readers, GIs who favored not only superheroes but more adult material. To cater to this audience Biro broke through the implied barriers that had existed up until then. While this allowed for more freedom it also, eventually, encouraged the excesses that came close to crippling the industry in the 1950s. The covers, Biro's only art contribution to the magazine, went in for bright and basic colors, violent drawings, and lots of hard-sell copy.

Mellowing, Biro eventually dropped the villains from *Boy* and *Daredevil* and began attacking juvenile delinquency and other social problems. He even tried, in the early 1950s, a kiddie comic called *Uncle Charlie's Fables.* He went to work for NBC as a graphic artist in 1962 and remained there until his death ten years later.

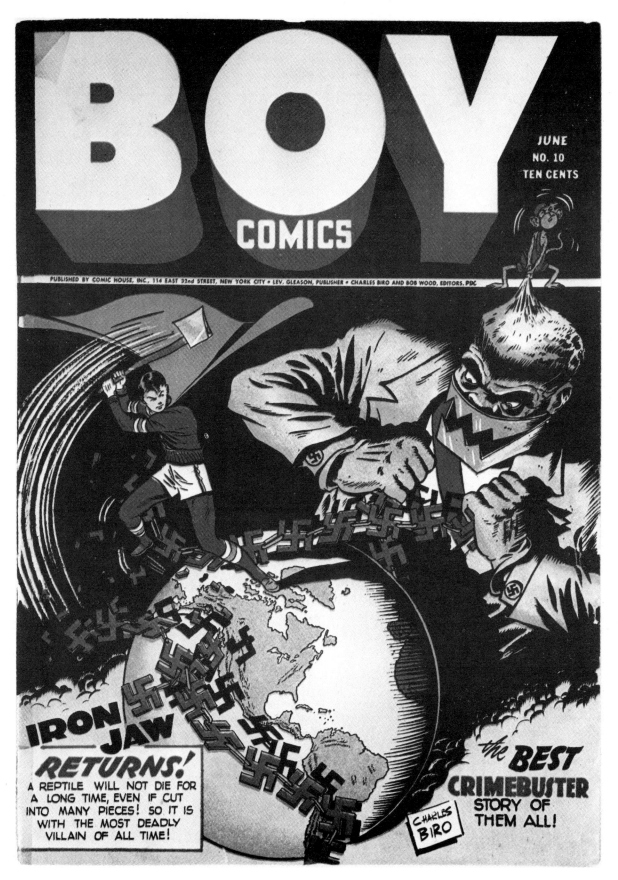

A typical hard-selling Biro cover, as compelling as a movie poster. *(Copyright © 1943 Comic House, Inc.)*

Dick Briefer

His specialty was monsters, both horrifying and whimsical. And he's best remembered for the nearly fifteen years he devoted to drawing everybody's favorite: the Frankenstein monster.

Although Briefer studied at Manhattan's Art Students League, he had originally intended to be a doctor. "NYU didn't agree with me on that," he once explained, "so their loss was Eisner and Iger's gain." He went to work in their shop in 1937 and in the following year his first monster appeared in the tabloid-size pages of *Jumbo Comics*. His *Hunchback of Notre Dame*—"suggested by Victor Hugo's great classic"—was a clumsy effort and owed more to Lon Chaney's silent movie version than it did to the novel. But it was a start for Briefer and the next time he borrowed from the movies he fared much better.

First, though, Briefer drew plenty of monsters, mostly of an extraterrestrial nature. Commencing with *Mystery Men Comics* #1 (August, 1939), he drew *Rex Dexter of Mars*. The alien creatures that blond Rex and his sweetheart Cynde encountered were mostly of the "hideous, blood-freezing" sort. So were those tangled with by Flint Baker over in *Planet Comics*. In the very first issue (January, 1940), for example, Baker came face to face with the one-eyed monster men of Mars. Briefer stuck with Flint for only five months, but drew Rex's interplanetary adventures for nearly two years. He also did one episode of the Human Top, a superhero with the dubious ability of being able to spin around real fast, for Marvel's *Red Raven Comics*. In later years he had no recollection of this whirligig crimebuster at all.

By the time Briefer introduced the Frankenstein monster in the seventh issue of *Prize Comics* (December, 1939), there had been three highly successful Frankenstein movies, each starring Boris Karloff. Briefer was obviously thinking of the actor when he created his version. Since the novel was public domain and Karloff wasn't, he was careful to state at the start of each comic book episode that it was "suggested by the classic of Mary Shelley." Updating the story, he gave it a contemporary American setting and showed his hulking, dead-white monster rampaging in streamlined urban settings. Within a few months Briefer began calling the monster Frankenstein, explaining, "the name is universally accepted to be that of the ghastly creation."

A man with a strong, though somewhat perverse, sense of humor, Briefer apparently soon tired of doing all the ghastly stuff straight. By the middle 1940s he had converted *Frankenstein* to a comedy feature. He kidded the whole horror genre, made fun of contemporary fads and foibles such as crooners and quiz shows. The monster soon became the star of *Prize* and in 1945 began appearing in a bimonthly of his own. Briefer afterwards admitted that the humorous Frankenstein was the favorite of all his comic book work. "I look back into the old comic mags of *Frankenstein*," he said, "and really marvel at most of the art and ideas and scripts that I turned out."

The forties was a busy decade for him. He drew *The Pirate Prince,* about a liberal buccaneer who specialized in preying on slave traders and freeing their captives, for *Silver Streak* and then for *Daredevil* from 1941 to 1945. He also did *Real American #1* for *Daredevil*. It was one of the few strips ever to feature an American Indian as a costumed crimefighter. In *Boy Comics* he was represented by Yankee Longago, a kid who traveled through time.

Under the pen name of Dick Floyd, he drew Pinky Rankin for the American Communist Party's newspaper *The Daily Worker*. An adventure strip with "a proletarian hero who took part in the struggle against the Nazis as an underground fighter in the occupied countries of Europe," it ran from 1942 until after the end of the Second World War. Some feel that Briefer's association with this particular project may have contributed to his leaving comics in the conservative 1950s.

The humorous Frankenstein ended in the late 1940s, but the character came back in the early 1950s in a new, grim version. Briefer's heart didn't seem to be in it. After comic books he worked at commercial art and then portrait painting until his death in the early 1980s.

He was a unique artist, one who most likely couldn't have found work at a later period. He was basically not an illustrator, but a cartoonist, a man with his own individual graphic shorthand for telling his stories. At his worst, his pages looked sloppy and hurried. But at his best, there was a grace and a liveliness to his stuff that made it fun to look at and read. His own appraisal of his work was quite accurate: "Most of the art was excellent, carefully but loosely done."

Briefer's humorous version of the Frankenstein monster drawn in his loose, compelling style. *(Copyright © 1947 Feature Publications, Inc.)*

John Buscema

Buscema worked at Marvel in the late 1940s and for most of the 1950s without attracting undue attention. He returned in 1966 and by the middle 1970s, following the abdication of Jack Kirby, had become one of Marvel's most popular artists. Primarily a penciller, he drew almost all the successful characters of the seventies—Captain America, Daredevil, Ka-Zar, X-Men, Ghost Rider, Fantastic Four, Avengers, and Conan. His style, integrating elements of Kirby, Gil Kane, and John Romita, became the Marvel standard for the decade—the house dressing, as it were.

He was born in 1927, studied at both the High School of Music and Art and the Pratt Institute, and did his first comic book work when he was in his early twenties. That was for Marvel, where he drew crime, horror, mystery, romance, science fiction, Western, and just about every other category to be found in the eclectic postwar comics field. In addition to Marvel, Buscema drew for Whitman-Gold Key in the 1950s, pencilling cowboy and Indian features, including Roy Rogers. He also found employment with Quality, St. John, and Ziff-Davis. For Charlton he did the odd and short-lived Nature Boy. By the time he got back to Marvel in the mid-sixties, after a spell in advertising, the superhero renaissance was underway, and he devoted much of his time to that genre. "When I went back . . . to superheroes," he's said, "it took me awhile before I got the feel of superheroes." Once he got the feel, though, it was smooth sailing. His earliest assignments included the Hulk, Sub-Mariner, and the Silver Surfer.

In 1973 he inherited America's best-loved barbarian when Barry Windsor-Smith left Conan for other things. "Buscema was expected to generate little excitement," says *The World Encyclopedia of Comics.* "But . . . he drew Conan in a pristine but exciting style that began accumulating a cult following all its own." He also drew the Robert E. Howard character frequently in *Savage Sword of Conan,* the black-and-white comic that commenced in 1974. Buscema was enthusiastic about this phase of his career. "I love the character," he once said. "I think it's a great character. I love the stories, I love the Howard stories."

Buscema tried his hand at a somewhat gentler type of material in 1979. That was with *Weirdworld,* Marvel's early attempt to invade the pixilated fantasy world of Wendy Pini's *Elfquest.* While the feature was not a success, it did give him an opportunity to demonstrate that he could function effectively in a realm other than that of the musclemen.

For a few years, he ran the John Buscema Comicbook Workshop in Manhattan. This led to the publication, in 1978, of *How To Draw Comics The Marvel Way,* in which "Buscema graphically illustrates the hitherto mysterious methods of comic art." With text by Stan Lee and artwork by Buscema, the book has gone into several editions. In the course of it Lee explains what the Marvel style and what the Buscema style are. "Action. A Marvel specialty!" says Lee. And exaggeration—"Thrusting the head farther forward, or spreading the legs farther apart, can make all the difference in the world." There is also a particular Marvel-Buscema way of composing panels and pages. Lee recommends thinking in terms of camera angles, adding, "Some camera angles are more dramatic, more interesting than others." For Buscema this means tilting your camera, shooting up from the floor or down from the rafters, zooming in for quirky close-ups.

Recently, Buscema has done some work on *Conan,* contributed to *Epic,* and resumed pencilling *Avengers.* If he hasn't been as prolific in the 1980s as he was earlier in his career, he's still one of Marvel's top artists.

John Buscema's muscular Conan prepares to do battle. Script by Roy Thomas, inks by Alfredo Alcala. *(Copyright © 1976 Marvel Comics Group.)*

John Byrne

After little more than a decade as a professional, Byrne has become one of the most popular artists in comic books. In 1985 the subscribers of the *Comics Buyer's Guide,* for example, voted him their favorite artist. And the two titles he drew and wrote—*Fantastic Four* and *Alpha Flight*—appeared on the CBG list of favorite comics. What he's managed to do is deliver work of quality without upsetting anybody. His pages look the way the majority of readers feels contemporary comic book pages ought to look. His style, built on what's been done in the past by the likes of Jack Kirby, Gil Kane, and Neal Adams, is an eminently acceptable mix of bravura complexity and storytelling clarity.

Born in England in 1950, Byrne grew up in Canada. The first comic books he collected were DCs, especially "anything with Superman in it." Then he came upon Marvel. "I still remember the first Marvel comic I bought—*Fantastic Four #5!*" he's recalled. "After that, my buying habits changed and I started picking up *Spider-Man, The Avengers, Sgt. Fury.* I had the first six issues of *The Hulk.*"

He studied at the Alberta College of Art, contributed work to school publications and fanzines. "I got into comics by dumb luck," he's claimed. "I was in the right place at the right time." His first professional work was done for Charlton, for editor Nick Cuti, in 1974—*Rog-2000, Space: 1999,* and *Wheelie and the Chopper Bunch.* Rog-2000 had originally been done for a fanzine. "Cuti saw it. He liked it," Bryne's explained. "He asked me if I wanted to do it as a back-up for *E-Man.* And it was the first time anybody had offered me any kind of professional work, so I took it." *Wheelie,* based on a Hanna-Barbera television show, was not done in Byrne's characteristic style but in one that followed TV animation. "It was my first real comic book—and I said, 'I'm going to do a Carl Barks number.'"

From Charlton he went to Marvel, taking on such assignments as *Iron Fist, Ghost Rider, Daredevil, Spider-Man,* and *The Avengers.* By 1980, after winning a number of fan awards, he was drawing *Captain America* and *X-Men.* Looking back on his career in that year, Byrne said, "When I started doing comics I realized that I didn't have the sense of power that, say, Jack Kirby has, or the understanding of anatomy that Gil Kane has. So, I decided that I'd try to make my work a little different—try to make it stand out because it was subtle, because an expression or pose or gesture had a certain degree of subtlety."

It was with *X-Men* that Byrne really rose to fame in comics. His contribution went beyond his pencilling (meticulously inked by Terry Austin) to a great deal of input into plot and characterization, particularly with regard to the fan-favorite characters Wolverine and Phoenix. Byrne's collaboration with writer Chris Claremont was hardly seamless, but the energy they both put into the title made the characters and story lines come alive. During this same period, Byrne briefly pencilled *Fantastic Four*—the very title that hooked him in his youth—and in 1981 he returned to the book as artist-writer. He's done some of his most ambitious and impressive stuff during this latest stint. He's since taken on a total revamping of comics' greatest legend—*Superman.*

Recently, in *Fantastic Four,* his own *Alpha Flight,* and *Hulk,* Byrne has been making an effort to modify his style. "I spent five years trying to draw like Neal Adams, and then I spent five years not trying to draw like Neal Adams," he's said. "And there was no point in any of that ten years I've been in the business that I spent any time trying to draw like me. So I sat down one day and said, 'How would I draw if I didn't draw like Neal or not like Neal?'" He feels his newest look shows some influence of the French artists. "I've always liked that look. Of course, my earliest influences are British, the old *Eagle* stuff. . . . The basic drawing is the same. It's the line quality, the use of light and shade that are changing."

Star-Lord makes a dramatic entrance, and Byrne takes modern comics by storm. Script by Chris Claremont, inks by Terry Austin. *(Copyright © 1977 Marvel Comics Group.)*

George Carlson

Although he was in his mid fifties when he got into comics and spent just seven years at it, George Carlson managed to make his mark. *A Smithsonian Book of Comic-Book Comics* reprints the work of just fifteen of the hundreds of cartoonists who flourished during the Golden Age. And Carlson is one of them. Coeditor Martin Williams goes so far as to call him "a kind of George Herriman for little children," adding, "I realize this is praise indeed."

Born in 1887, George Leonard Carlson had a long career as a cartoonist, illustrator, and puzzle-maker prior to venturing into comic books. Even before the First World War he was already doing gag cartoons plus an occasional color cover for *Judge*. Carlson produced numerous puzzle, riddle, and alphabet books for children's publishers such as Platt & Munk and even illustrated some Uncle Wiggily stories. He concocted puzzles of all sorts—labyrinths, anagrams, etc.—for kids' magazines. For a time he was an instructor for a mail-order cartoon course and he produced more than one book on how to draw cartoons. Most of this earlier material is competent but traditional, hardly hinting at the wacky side of his personality that comic books unleashed.

Just about all of Carlson's comic book work was done for a single magazine—*Jingle Jangle Comics*. Edited by Steve Douglas and published by the same folks who'd brought forth the pioneering *Famous Funnies*, it came along in 1942 and stayed in business until near the end of 1949. In its forty-some issues it presented a mixture of funny animals, funny kids, and fantasy, mostly drawn in animated cartoon style. It also featured, in almost every issue, a dozen or more pages of George Carlson.

He was a one man band of a cartoonist—scripting, lettering, pencilling, inking, the works. Carlson held forth in two features—*Jingle Jangle Tales* and *The Pie-Face Prince of Old Pretzleburg*. It's safe to say nothing similar had been seen in comic books before. He mixed burlesque, fantasy, and word play into his own individual brand of nonsense, ending up with material that resembled a cockeyed cross between Lewis Carroll's *Alice* books and Olsen & Johnson's slapstick *Hellzapoppin* review. He took a streetwise, Broadway approach to fairy tales, turning out multilevel stuff in which the visual and the verbal worked together. The dialogue in his *Jingle Jangle* work demonstrates Carlson's fascination with language, with cooking up left-handed puns, and with twisting stock phrases into new and unexpected shapes. Quite obviously he was amusing himself first and foremost. And, like Walt Kelly, he had in mind not only the kids who were buying the comic books but the grownups who were going to be dragooned into reading his tales to them.

Among the characters who did turns in Carlson's *Jingle Jangle Tales* were the Youthful Yodeler, who lived on a newly painted mountain and sold all kinds of weather by the yard; the Very Horseless Jockey, who became rich from a flavored snowball business and then set out, via steamed-up steam engine, to buy a fine mahogany horse for himself; the Half-Champion Archer, who wasn't full-time champ because he could never hit the king's special Tuesday target. There were all sorts of other unusual props, people, and creatures to be found wandering through Carlson's lively, cluttered pages, such as a freshly toasted sandwich board, a young idea "with its buttons all neatly sewed on the wrong side," a four-footed yardstick maker, a zigzag zither, a lovely blond mazurka, and a trio of jellybeans, "all slicked up, with shoe-laces neatly pressed," who go forth into the world to seek their fortune.

Pretzleburg, ruled over by King Hokum without much help from his pie-face offspring Prince Dimwitri, was similar in appearance and politics to the various light-opera countries and locations to be found in the *Tales*. The recurrent players included Princess Panetella Murphy, who was more or less the object of Dimwitri's affections and could sometimes be found residing in "her left-footed uncle's second-best castle"; the Raging Rajah, billed as the Prince's "favorite enemy"; and the Wicked Green Witch. Prince Dimwitri's interests and adventures were wide-ranging. In one issue he set out to win the coveted Doopsniggle Prize with his corn-beef-flavored cabbage plant; in another he went aloft in an eighteen-karat balloon in search of a missing bass drum.

Carlson also produced, in 1946, two issues of *Puzzle Fun Comics*. An oddity, it consisted mostly of puzzle pages—mazes, rebuses, crosswords, word ladders, etc. Each issue also contained a six-page tale entitled *Alec in Fumbleland*. Starring a blond curly-haired young fellow named Alec Snigglewit and mixing melodrama parodies with characters out of *Alice in Wonderland*, these are much tamer than his *Jingle Jangle* work. He left comic books at the end of the forties, returning to illustrating. Among the children's books he illuminated were several in the Uncle Wiggily series. Carlson died in 1962.

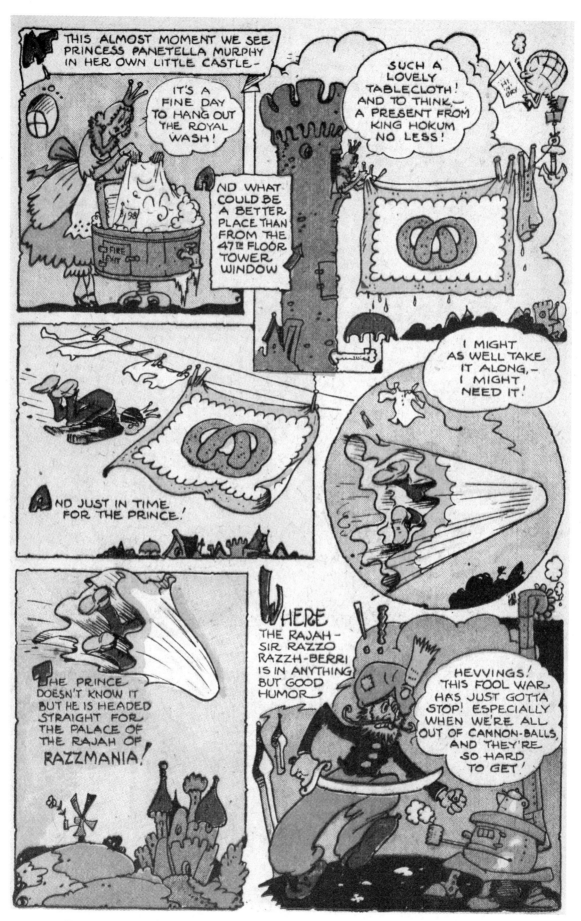

Romance, action, and violence, seen as only Carlson could see them. *(Copyright © 1944 Famous Funnies, Inc.)*

Howard Chaykin

Thus far Chaykin is the only comic book artist to have his work nominated for a Nebula award of the Science Fiction Writers of America. That happened in 1985, when three episodes from his *American Flagg!* were nominated in the best short story category. None won, but still the thought was there. Nineteen eighty-five was also the year Chaykin made an admirable showing in the poll conducted by the *Comics Buyer's Guide.* He came in fifth in the favorite artist category, seventh in favorite writer. *American Flagg!* placed seventh on the favorite comic list, Reuben Flagg himself was seventh on the favorite character list, and Raul the talking cat from the Flagg cast easily took first-place honors for favorite supporting character. Chaykin returned to regular comic book work in 1983 with *American Flagg!,* after a two-year absence, and the move seems to have been a wise one.

From the moment it was launched, his far-from-utopian science fiction saga attracted favorable comments and substantial sales. Writing in *The Comics Journal* in the fall of 1983, the astute Heidi MacDonald said, *"American Flagg!* is snappy, snazzy and a hell of a lot of fun." She went on to say, "Each page or panel is carefully designed as a graphic unit, and the story moves along as much through the juxtaposition of elements in each unit as through the traditional panel-to-panel continuity." Her summation was that Chaykin displayed "a brilliantly unique personal vision."

Chaykin brought considerable enthusiasm to the project. "I feel like my brain and my body are like a phoenix rising from the ashes," he said shortly before the first issue appeared. "I have finally found a subject and theme and stories that are making my juices flow. I'm disgustingly enthusiastic about the strip." During the years he'd been away from comics, working in paperbacks, he'd become "soured very much on what was being done in American comics." When approached by First Comics to develop a comic book of his own, Chaykin was certain he didn't want to do a Marvel-type book —"I love the idea of comics, but I'm not very interested in superheroes." He also felt "that comics need more humor than they have." He came up with his futuristic lawman, Reuben Flagg, and "what I consider a fairly

provocative adventure and entertainment strip . . . It's thrills, chills, and laughs, like *Plastic Man* by Jack Cole." Chaykin is also concerned with reaching an audience that is somewhat older than the one comics are usually assumed to be aimed at. "I've got a particular desire to hold on to people after their hormones go to hell," he says, "and stay there with the material. . . . I'm trying to introduce some stuff that I have not seen in comics before."

In *American Flagg!* Chaykin has utilized just about everything he's learned and developed since breaking into comics in the early 1970s. His breakdowns are expert, mixing movie techniques, European comic book tricks, and his own personal ideas very well. His drawing has improved steadily over the years until his figure work, perspectives, and overall rendering can't be faulted. While not yet an equal of his idol, Jack Cole, Chaykin is still very good at blending action, adventure, and comedy. His scripts don't quite match his artwork —"Chaykin isn't as adroit a writer as he is an artist," is how MacDonald puts it—but he's still several notches above much of the current competition.

It was in 1972 that Chaykin began his career, starting out at Marvel and then moving over to DC. He did an adaptation of *Star Wars* for Marvel and worked on DC's short-lived *Sword of Sorcery* and the even shorter-lived *Scorpion* for Atlas. For Star*Reach he produced *Cody Starbuck,* another SF opus. One of the earlier high points of his career was a graphic novel adaptation of Alfred Bester's *The Stars My Destination.* More recently he drew some striking covers for DC's *Blackhawk.*

While he is working on other projects, including a recent *Shadow* miniseries for DC, Chaykin is still guiding the exploits of Reuben Flagg. "I'm convinced this is my first major adult work," he's said. "This is not to eliminate my last twelve years' output, but it is to say that I have never felt as comfortable with a character, with a situation, and with a circumstance as I have now." As for what his readers can expect of him, Chaykin has promised, "The same wonderful combination of snotty dialogue, nasty characters, venal attitudes, petty motivations, and sex and violence, with a bit of my new-found prejudices."

Swordplay and heroics with Dominic Fortune, done in Chaykin's inimitable style. Script by Len Wein. *(Copyright © 1979 Marvel Comics Group.)*

Gene Colan

During his forty-some years in comics Gene Colan has drawn a great many superheroes, including Sub-Mariner, Captain America, and Batman. There are those who agree with *The World Encyclopedia of Comics* that "his most recognizable work has been in the superhero field" and that "Colan draws incredibly handsome figures in majestic poses." Colan himself, however, has never been especially fond of them and has always had more fun elsewhere. "I'd like to get away from superheroes," he's said, "I'd like to get into just plain storytelling." One of his favorite projects in recent years was Marvel's *Tomb of Dracula,* a book wherein he could concentrate on storytelling rather than superheroic poses.

Born in the Bronx in 1926, he grew up in Manhattan. He discovered newspaper strips early in life and his favorite was *Dickie Dare,* begun by Milton Caniff and carried on by Coulton Waugh. "I would meet my father with such anticipation and anxiety at the subway," he recalls. "I couldn't wait for him to come up out of the subway so I could grab the paper out of his hand . . . and right out there on the street I'd open to the comics page to see what happened to Dickie Dare."

Although he attended art school, Colan doesn't think he learned much that was practical there. He broke into comics at Fiction House in 1944, drawing for *Wings Comics.* Appropriately enough, he then entered the air force. After the war he resumed his efforts and landed a job with Marvel. "We all sat in a big room called the Bullpen. Syd Shores overlooked everyone because he was the oldest member, the one with the most experience. We were all kids at the time. Within a week John Buscema came along and he became part of the team."

He worked in every category for a variety of companies, as the comic book business waxed and waned in the fifties and sixties. His cinematically designed pages —favoring odd angles, quirky close-ups and lighting that brought out deep shadows—were to be found in war books, romance books, and such horror books as *Menace, Mystic,* and *Journey into Mystery.* Colan also worked for DC in these decades, turning out everything from *Sea Devils* to *Hopalong Cassidy.* He wasn't especially fond of this latter assignment. "The artist had no leeway," he's said. "He wasn't even allowed to sign his name to the stories. Each panel was written out. I felt like I was a student when I was finished because I would come in with the work and I would show it to the editor and he would go over it."

When the superheroes began their comeback in the 1960s, Colan returned to Marvel. He handled a batch of them—Daredevil, Sub-Mariner, Iron Man, Silver Surfer, Dr. Strange, etc. Dracula is hard to kill and in the early 1970s he began flapping his wings for Marvel. When Colan heard of the plans to launch a Dracula comic, he campaigned enthusiastically to get the job. Although frightened by monster films as a child, he was also fascinated by them—"I was drawn to horror movies like a fly to flypaper." He got the assignment and, with most of the scripts by Marv Wolfman, went on to draw *Tomb of Dracula,* for all of its seventy-issue life. The book was quite successful and, in the opinion of *Amazing Heroes,* Colan "turned out some of his greatest, moodiest work on the feature." He also served some time with *Howard the Duck,* both in comic book and newspaper strips formats.

The 1980s found Colan once again at DC. Teaming again with Wolfman, he tried another horror book, *The Night Force.* The critical reaction was mostly favorable —"His brooding, shadowy style, often termed impressionistic, seems especially well-suited to this material . . . and every so often he subtly captures the emotional mood of a character with a moving precision that is rare indeed in comics," said *The Comics Journal*—but the magazine succumbed in 1983, after just fourteen issues. More recently Colan's been occupied with the Batman feature in *Detective Comics,* and with various miniseries and maxiseries. He drew the twelve-issue *Jemm, Son of Saturn* series and, thus far, two four-issue series of *Nathaniel Dusk, Private Investigator*—"This is an honest man. That makes him as good as dead." The first miniseries about the 1930s private eye got mixed reviews and only fair sales. The artwork was reproduced from Colan's pencils, with no inking. More recently, he has completed an adaptation of Robert Silverberg's award-winning *Nightwings.*

Colan continues to work, undaunted. "I like to tell a story once and then move on to another thing," he's said. "Each story ought to be a challenge in itself and not go back and repeat what you've already done."

Colan's Dracula displays both his strength and his hypnotic prowess. Script by Marv Wolfman, inks by Bob McLeod. *(Copyright © 1979 Marvel Comics Group.)*

Jack Cole

Jack Cole was born in 1914 and killed himself in 1958, four months shy of his forty-fourth birthday. In the spring of his last year, already the star gag cartoonist of the increasingly popular *Playboy,* he sold a comic strip to the Chicago Sun-Times Syndicate. It was titled *Betsy and Me,* and Cole provided some third-person autobiography to be sent out with the publicity for it. He said, "The artist's life (it's not yet completed). Jack Cole was born in 1914 in New Castle, Pa. At 15, he took the Landon School of Cartooning mail correspondence course. Highlights of his career thus far are: 1932, a 7,000 mile bicycle trip to California and return. 1933, graduated from high school. 1934, married Dorothy Mahoney. 1934, got a job at American Can Factory and started mailing out cartoons to magazines. 1935, first sale to *Boy's Life.* 1936, borrowed $500 in small amounts from home town merchants and set out with his wife for New York to find cartoon work. 1937–'54, worked for comic magazines. 1954, free-lance cartooning. 1955, lost nearly all of his furniture and belongings in the New England floods. 1958, 43 years old, 24 years married."

His comic book career, which Cole dismissed in four words, was one of the most impressive ever and Cole is one of the few comic book artists to be referred to, both by fans and by his colleagues, as a genius. Cole really wanted, however, to be a successful gag cartoonist.

Settled in a small apartment in Manhattan and unable to sell many of his cartoons or get paid for the ones he did manage to sell, he decided to try the comic book business. Cole first found work in the Chesler shop, drawing mostly humorous filler pages. By 1940 he was doing more or less straight superhero stuff, such as *The Comet* in *Pep Comics* and *Daredevil* in *Silver Streak.* The following year he signed on with the Quality line.

For *Smash Comics,* starting in #18 (January, 1941), he created *Midnight.* A fellow who fought crime in a business suit, snap-brim hat and mask, Midnight was something of a Spirit surrogate. But since Cole and Eisner were original and inventive fellows, the two features developed in different directions. While both men refused to take the profession of masked crimefighter completely seriously, Eisner became more interested in urban melodramas while Cole pursued fantasy and science fiction and, on occasion, a somewhat bizarre approach to violence. He had the advantage over many of his contemporaries in that he could write as well as draw. He knew how to tell an entertaining story in comic book terms and how to package it.

Cole's artwork made a leap ahead with Midnight. His line became finer, more assured, and his layouts and staging grew even more inventive and audacious. Cole's interest in movies and animated cartoons shows in his work. The time and attention he was lavishing on his Quality pages would eventually cause him deadline problems, but he was having an obvious good time exploring the possibilities of the comic book medium.

Plastic Man first bounced into view in *Police Comics* # 1 (August, 1941). Cole wrote his own blurb for the initial yarn, proclaiming, "From time to time the comic book world welcomes a new sensation! Such is PLASTIC MAN!! The most fantastic man alive!" With *Plastic Man* Cole had a feature where he could make use of all the skills he'd been developing. His narratives mixed fantasy, cops and robbers, violence, and humor. His drawing style, a blend of the straight approach and the exaggerations of animated cartoons, was ideally suited to depicting Plas's adventures. While the strip is sometimes described as a satire on other superguys, it wasn't really that at all. What Cole was turning out, in the first years anyway, was closer to what was being done in the movies of the time. He was producing his own mystery-comedies.

Throughout the 1940s, while Cole was producing adventure and superhero material, he was also drawing a good deal of out-and-out funny stuff, most of it in the one-page-filler category. For *Smash* there was the Oriental detective *Wun Cloo. Dan Tootin* ran in *Hit, Windy Breeze* in *National,* and *Burp the Twerp* in *Police.* Burp the Twerp, billed as the Super So-and-So, was bald and had a shaggy white moustache and a body like an overripe balloon. Cole used him to poke fun at the more sober-sided supermen as well as his own Plastic Man. All of his humor pages were signed with the penname Ralph Johns.

Cole came to the attention of *Playboy* in the middle 1950s. His full-page gags, often done in bright watercolor, soon became staples of the magazine. When, in 1955, Hugh Hefner suggested that he relocate in the Chicago area, Cole was less than enthusiastic. But the money offered was very good and he and his wife made the move. He maintained he didn't miss the comic book business at all. In fact, when Quality tried to hire him back, Cole replied he wasn't interested and "that I was going to be the best damn cartoonist" in the gag field. And he was very successful with *Playboy.*

Early in 1958 another of his long-time dreams came true when he sold his comic strip. A few months later he was dead.

Unlike some of his contemporaries, Cole was obviously having fun with superheroics.
(Copyright © 1940 Your Guide Publications.)

Reed Crandall

Quite a few comic book artists, especially in the early days, looked no further than the funny papers, to Roy Crane, Alex Raymond, and Milton Caniff, for their inspiration. Reed Crandall was wider ranging, as well as more gifted, than many of his contemporaries. He was one of the artists—Lou Fine was another—who assimilated the techniques of earlier book and magazine illustrators and applied them to the drawing of comic book pages. In Crandall's case the admired illustrators included Herbert Morton Stoops, Henry C. Pitz, and Howard Pyle.

Although undoubtedly one of the most technically proficient artists in comics, and a master at drawing the figure in action, Crandall was associated with few out-and-out winners in his long career. His two biggest successes—Dollman and Blackhawk—occurred in the 1940s.

A Midwesterner, he arrived in New York in 1940 and worked first for the Eisner-Iger shop and then directly for the Quality comics line. Everett "Busy" Arnold, Quality publisher, later called him "the best man I ever had," and he saw to it that Crandall was kept busy. He drew Stormy Foster and Hercules for *Hit Comics,* Uncle Sam for *National,* Captain Triumph for *Crack.* Crandall was also intended to have the star spot in *Police Comics,* with the Firebrand, "the mysterious figure who fights for justice." In civilian life the Firebrand was Rod Reilly, another of those millionaire playboys who turned to crimefighting because of boredom with his ritzy life. What saved this Wall Street do-gooder from being a complete dud was Crandall's artwork, which endowed the rather stodgy stories with a bit more excitement and life than they actually deserved. But neither Crandall nor Firebrand were any match for Jack Cole and Plastic Man. Cole's flexible superhero began in the back of *Police,* but within a year it was the undisputed champ. Crandall took over Dollman, the teeny-weeny good guy invented by Eisner and drawn initially by Fine, in *Feature Comics* #44 (May, 1941). He did an impressive job, particularly in depicting the seemingly giant props—fountain pens, briefcases, chairs, mice, bell jars, etc.—his diminutive hero worked amidst. Another second-banana

hero he inherited from Fine was the yellow-suited Ray. He drew him from the summer of 1941 until just before his demise early in 1943.

The high point of his efforts at Quality was Blackhawk. Crandall first drew Blackhawk and his band of mercenaries in *Military Comics* #12 (October, 1942). The feature was yet another Eisner creation. Charles Cuidera, working from Eisner roughs, was the original artist, and just prior to Crandall Alex Kotzky was handling the drawing. In fact, Kotzky is also responsible for four of the pages in Crandall's eleven-page debut yarn. Thereafter Crandall was *the* Blackhawk artist, doing many of the covers and most of the stories. When a *Blackhawk* comic book began in 1944, he was there as well. More realistic here than he had been on the Ray or Dollman, Crandall seemed to relish drawing the nasty Axis villains, the sultry ladies who were not to be trusted, and the many weapons, planes, gadgets, and engines of destruction that were required. He also excelled at the complicated battle scenes, whether they involved bazookas and flame throwers or hand-to-hand combat.

After Quality folded in the early 1950s, Crandall migrated to EC. He drew just about every sort of story there, including horror, crime, science fiction, pirates, and war. William Gaines, the EC headman, said of his advent, "He came walking in one day and of course we all had heard of Reed Crandall and we were just as impressed with him as he was with us. So we fell on each other's necks and he became part of the group immediately. He was a fine, fine craftsman and did some of our very best stuff." In the 1960s he worked for *Classics Illustrated,* for *Treasure Chest,* the Catholic comic book, and for the *Twilight Zone* comic. He also contributed frequently to *Creepy* and *Eerie.* Crandall's style grew stiffer and colder over the years and much of his later work, especially that in the Warren black-and-whites, was the sort that inspired admiration but not engagement—art that made you feel as though you were in a museum and ought to step back while murmuring admiringly.

Crandall produced little or no work in his final years, which were touched with illness and personal problems. He died in the autumn of 1982.

A handsome example of Crandall's work from the fifties. *(Copyright © 1986 William M. Gaines.)*

Jack Davis

One of the most successful commercial cartoonists in the country, Davis feels he owes much of his current status to the fact that he was a featured contributor to the EC comic books of the 1950s. He once explained that many of the ad agency art directors who contact him nowadays were kids back then and still have fond memories of his work in the EC war and horror titles and, especially, in *Mad.*

Davis was born in Atlanta, Georgia, in 1926. By the time he was in his early teens he was certain he wanted to be a cartoonist and he was already sending his work out to the various kid-oriented publications that had a page set aside for amateur artists. *Tip Top Comics,* among others, printed these early Davis efforts. While attending the University of Georgia he contributed to the campus newspaper and also helped found an off-campus humor magazine titled *Bullsheet*—"Not political or anything, but just something with risqué jokes and cartoons." While in college Davis also spent a summer working as inker on Ed Dodd's *Mark Trail* newspaper strip.

He headed east in about 1950—"All the syndicates and major publishers are in New York. Atlanta didn't have any of that." His first job was with the New York Herald Tribune Syndicate, inking Mike Roy's *The Saint* strip. From there Davis moved into comic books. "I went around to all the comic book publishers and I was turned down so many times," he later recalled, "and then I was accepted at EC." He arrived at EC soon after several of their innovative titles—*Tales From The Crypt, Weird Fantasy, Two-Fisted Tales,* and *Vault of Horror*— were launched. He did some impressive work for them, in a style that was almost straight but didn't quite hide Davis's cartoony leanings. "I'm a cartoonist," he admits, "not an illustrator." In 1952 came *Mad,* cooked up for EC by Harvey Kurtzman. It was basically a college humor magazine in comic book form—less raunchy but with a similar irreverent and wacky outlook—and in its pages Davis came into his own. He perfected a loose, scratchy approach, displaying an admirable knack for exaggerated expressions of both faces and body. He also showed himself to be a crackerjack caricaturist, an ability that would win him a good many jobs in the future.

Less admirable was some of the work Davis turned out for the EC horror titles. "I enjoyed doing the horror bit and they liked it," he's said, adding, "I think it was pretty bad. At the time, I didn't realize how bad it was —but now that I look back, I know it was." Davis' most memorable effort in the horror genre was a story called "Foul Play." In it a nasty ball player gets his comeuppance by being dismembered by his teammates and having his parts used in a ball game—his head for the ball, arm for a bat, intestines to mark the base lines, etc. *Foul Play* had two of its most explicit panels reprinted in Frederic Wertham's *Seduction of the Innocent.* Robert Warshow, in a famous essay on horror comics that originally appeared in *Commentary,* discusses it unfavorably and concludes, "I don't suppose I shall easily forget that baseball game."

Davis stopped doing this sort of thing in the fifties and has been able to concentrate on humorous work ever since. Unlike some of his colleagues, he has had many disciples. And several lesser artists have enjoyed moderately rewarding careers by imitating him. Although he never completely deserted comic books and has continued to work for *Mad* and some of its imitators, the majority of his work has been in other areas: for bubble gum cards, children's games, *Time* covers, *TV Guide* covers, and numerous advertising clients. Discussing his career recently Davis said, "There have been a lot of thrills, a lot of happiness."

The style that just about every advertising art director came to love while growing up.
(Copyright © 1986 William M. Gaines.)

Steve Ditko

When you're in at the creation of one of the most successful characters in the half-century history of comic books, it's sometimes difficult to know what to do for an encore. To some extent this has been Ditko's problem. The high point of his career was his involvement with Spider-Man in the sixties. In the intervening years he's drawn a wide range of stuff—from straight superheroes to adaptations of TV shows to espousals of his personal philosophy—without ever equalling the impact he achieved with Spidey.

He was born in Johnstown, Pennsylvania, a hamlet famous for its flood, in 1927. Ditko studied at Manhattan's Cartoonists and Illustrators School, where Jerry Robinson was one of his instructors. In the early 1950s, a period when superheroes were not faring especially well, Ditko broke into comics. A man with an apparent fondness for fantasy and horror, his early work was for such magazines as *Black Magic, Strange Suspense Stories,* and *Fantastic Fears,* which offered its breathless readers "tales of stalking terror." His style was not as sure then, owing quite a bit to the EC artists of the time. Eventually Ditko developed his own individual drawing style, influenced by both Joe Kubert and Jack Kirby.

In 1956 he undertook *Tales of the Mysterious Traveler* for Charlton. It showed a certain amount of enterprise on Charlton's part to base a comic book on a radio show that had gone off the air for good four years earlier. *The Mysterious Traveler,* which first came to radio in 1943, was the Mutual network's answer to such crime and creeps shows as *Inner Sanctum, The Whistler,* and *Suspense.* The comic book version brought out some of Ditko's best drawing to date.

By the late 1950s Ditko was working for Marvel, helping the likes of Kirby, Everett, and Don Heck fill the haunted, monster-ridden pages of *Tales of Suspense, Amazing Adventures, Journey Into Mystery,* etc. His work of this period won him many fans and is still fondly recalled. Writing in *Comics Collector,* Will Murray has said, "My favorite of the Marvel crew had to be Steve Ditko. In those days he inked his own pencils in a creepy, crepuscular style. . . . If Kirby was King of

Monsters, Steve Ditko was the Emir of Aliens."

The sixties was the decade that saw the triumphant revival of the superheroes—Fantastic Four in 1961, Thor in 1962, Daredevil in 1964. Ditko had gotten there ahead of the pack, creating Captain Atom for Charlton's *Space Adventures* very early in 1960, but the blond captain only made it through ten issues before being shut down. Ditko's next hero fared considerably better. Spider-Man, the joint invention of Stan Lee, Kirby, and Ditko, made his debut in *Amazing Fantasy* #15 (September, 1962). The magazine expired with that issue, but Spidey, having achieved impressive sales figures, returned in his own *The Amazing Spider-Man* early the next year. Ditko established the look of the major characters—Peter Parker, Aunt May, J. Jonah Jameson—and the villains—Dr. Octopus, the Vulture, the Green Goblin, Kraven, etc. He also worked out his own personal version of New York City as a setting for Spider-Man's urban crime busting activities. His drawing became a bit more cartoony, emphasizing the less-than-reverent attitude that Lee's scripts took toward the profession of superhero.

During this same period Ditko was also working on the Hulk, and in 1963 he created Dr. Strange for *Strange Tales.* This latter feature, in the words of historian Joe Brancatelli, "afforded him the opportunity to introduce intricate worlds of mysticism and intrigue." After a falling out with Marvel in 1966, he went on to produce pages for a variety of other publishers. For Dell there was *Get Smart* and *Hogan's Heroes;* for DC *Creeper* and *The Hawk and the Dove.* He drew for the Warren black-and-whites and turned out *Mr. A.*—which dealt in a didactic fashion with his notions about life and the ongoing conflict between good and evil—for magazines like *Witzend.*

Those interested in the current Ditko output will find him back in the Marvel fold again. Most recently he's been working on such titles as *Indiana Jones* and *Rom* as a penciller. Those interested in his earlier activities have but to check out recent issues of *Marvel Tales,* where his original Spidey yarns from two decades ago have been reprinted.

Ditko's classic Spider-Man, striking characteristic poses in both his identities. Script by Stan Lee. *(Copyright © 1965 Marvel Comics Group.)*

Will Eisner

An entrepreneur as well as an artist, Eisner has fared much better than most of his fellow pioneers—both financially and in terms of lasting reputation. The Spirit, a character he owns outright, is still going strong in reprints all over the world, and to fans as well as critics and historians, Eisner is one of the undisputed geniuses of the comic book field. Eclectic in approach, Eisner mixed elements from the movies, the stage, radio, literature, and the corner pool room into *The Spirit.* He also had a hand in the creation of such comics perennials as Sheena and Blackhawk.

Born in Brooklyn in 1917, Eisner was selling his work to comics before he was out of his teens. By the time he was twenty-one he was, in partnership with Jerry Iger, running a shop to provide material for the burgeoning comic book industry. "We started a factory producing comics in a tiny little office on Madison Avenue," he's recalled. "The concept of the studio was to be a packager, to produce the entire insides of a comic book, and sell it to a publisher who would then publish it." The early staff included Dick Briefer, Jack Kirby, Bob Powell, and Lou Fine. "The shop was run pretty much the way a Roman Galley ship operates. I sat at the end of a long row of sweating artists."

Among the first clients were T. T. Scott's Fiction House line and the incomparable Victor Fox's group of titles. Eisner drew covers for such magazines as *Jumbo Comics*—home of Sheena, Queen of the Jungle—*Planet,* and *Wonderworld.* His swashbuckling pirate saga *Hawks of the Sea* appeared in *Jumbo,* and for *Wonderworld,* after his Wonder Man folded up rather than face DC's wrath, he drew *Yarko the Great.* A more fruitful, and lucrative, association was the one he formed with Everett "Busy" Arnold. For Arnold's Quality group Eisner drew *Espionage* in *Smash Comics* and cooked up the tiny superhero Dollman, illustrated by Lou Fine, for *Feature.* After parting with Iger, Eisner undertook the editing of Quality's *National* and *Military.* He wrote and drew the initial adventures of the superpatriot Uncle Sam for *National* and invented Blackhawk and his gang, drawn initially by Chuck Cuidera, for *Military.* And it was while associated with Arnold that he created *The Spirit.*

As the forties began comic books were selling in the millions. This had not gone unnoticed by newspapers and syndicates. *Superman* had branched out into a newspaper strip in 1939, and by the following year readyprint comic books were being offered for insertion in Sunday papers. The enterprising Victor Fox tried to launch one, the Chicago *Tribune* introduced a *Comic Book Magazine,* and the Register & Tribune Syndicate, a silent partner to Busy Arnold, brought forth a sixteen-page weekly *Spirit* booklet. In addition to Eisner's hero it featured *Lady Luck,* originally drawn by Chuck Mazoujian, and Bob Powell's *Mr. Mystic.* Although the Spirit somewhat resembled a traditional comic book character, he differed sharply from the brightly costumed superheroes to be found leaping and bounding through the numerous comic books crowding the newsstands. For one thing, he refused to take his profession seriously. "Sartorically the Spirit was miles from the other masked heroes," Jules Feiffer has pointed out in *The Great Comic Book Heroes.* "He didn't wear tights, just a baggy blue business suit, a wide-brimmed blue hat that needed blocking, and, for a disguise, a matching blue eye mask." Feiffer feels that Eisner's characters were "identifiable by that look of just having got off the boat. The Spirit reeked of lower middle-class; his nose may have turned up, but we all knew he was Jewish."

Eisner quite obviously learned on the job, and had a great deal of fun doing it. His stories got better, trickier and less melodramatic, and his layouts moved further and further away from the traditional. Nobody's ever equalled him in incorporating his logo into the splash panel, and a few have come close to capturing the look and feel, the shadows and smells, of urban life.

Eisner entered the service in 1942, turning *The Spirit* over to others—chiefly Lou Fine. Attached to the Ordnance Department, he did considerable drawing and developed an abiding interest in "educational and industrial cartooning." He resumed working on *The Spirit* in 1945 and, aided by such artists as John Spranger, Jerry Grandenetti, Wally Wood, and Feiffer, turned out six more years of memorable strips. Although the *Spirit* material appearing in the current magazine is reprinted, Eisner still gets to draw his baggypants hero on the magazine's new covers. He's also doing new work for *Will Eisner's Quarterly* and continues to produce graphic novels—*A Contract With God, Life Force,* etc.

"No one ever had to tell him how good he was and now that he is being told again and again, he is amenable but hardly impressed," says Feiffer. "He remains ambitious and competitive, a cartoonist not out of the past but an artist who encompasses past, present and, very probably, future."

Eisner was able to come up with an imaginative opening page like this week after week.
(Copyright © 1986 Will Eisner.)

Lee Elias

The leading exponent of the Milton Caniff approach in comic books, Elias broke into the field in 1943. His two most successful forties characters were feisty ladies, both of them redheads—Firehair, the Western heroine he created for *Rangers Comics* in 1945, and Black Cat, the Hollywood star turned crimefighter that he took over in 1946. In the ensuing decades he drew in all sorts of categories, including science fiction, horror, and superheroes.

Leopold Elias was born in England in 1920. He came to America in his youth, settled in New York City, and spent eight years studying the violin. "I loved the fiddle but couldn't eat it," he's said, "so I studied art at Cooper Union and the Art Students League." His earliest work was done for Fiction House, where he applied his variation of Caniff's impressionist style to a number of aviation strips—*Suicide Smith, Captain Wings,* and *Phantom Falcon*—in *Wings Comics. The World Encyclopedia of Comics,* in its entry on him, is quite taken with this aspect of his work. It says, "Elias's lovingly rendered airplanes were among the finest of the time." He also drew his first science fiction strips for *Planet Comics. Firehair* was done for Fiction House and was the first hit character he was associated with.

Elias began drawing *Black Cat* with the second issue of her bimonthly (August–September, 1946). His work had been improving rapidly and he brought a sophisticated, slick look to the adventures of "Hollywood's Glamorous Detective Star." Red-haired Linda Turner was a famous movie actress by day and a sparsely costumed crimefighter by night. Elias was deft at drawing her in both her roles and was also good with all the hardware, from movie cameras to motorcycles, that was called for. He stuck with the magazine for several years, seeing it through the various changes the Harvey Brothers put it through while trying to outguess the public taste. The magazine was known, in various phases, as *Black Cat Western, Black Cat Mystery, Black Cat Mystic,* and *Black Cat Western Mystery.* The Black Cat herself, once "The Darling of the Comics," was dropped in the early 1950s and the book went on without her, offering a collection of weird tales each issue. At this same time Elias was drawing superheroes for a variety of publishers. He did Sub-Mariner for Marvel, the Flash for DC.

A bright spot in the history of science fiction strips and one of the best things Elias ever did was *Beyond Mars.* It appeared as a Sunday page, running only in the New York *News.* But since the *Sunday News* was sold on newsstands all across the country, the strip could be said to have had a national circulation. It began in 1952 and ran until 1955. The scripts were by veteran science fiction writer Jack Williamson. Using his novels about Seetee—CT stood for contraterrene, better known these days as antimatter—as a basis, Williamson invented a tabloid page starring Mike Flint, a "licensed spatial engineer," who lived two hundred and some years in the future on Brooklyn Rock in the asteroid belt. It was a time when "a new force—paragravity—had enabled men to live and breathe on the asteroids." Elias did an excellent job of illustration and the strip was a fast-moving adventure feature with touches of real science fiction and real humor.

Returning to comic books after the demise of *Beyond Mars,* Elias worked again for DC from the late 1950s into the 1970s. He was able to indulge his interest in science fiction with characters like Tommy Tomorrow. There were costumed crimefighters and superheroes, too—Eclipso, Green Arrow, Automan—plus assorted weird tales. His output slowed in the 1970s and for some years he lived again in his native England. He contributed an SF strip called *Kronos* to a short-lived independent publication of Joe Kubert's and did some handsome black-and-white work for the Warren publications. Elias drew the title character in *The Rook,* a B&W magazine that lasted for seven issues before folding late in 1980. Restin Dane, a.k.a. the Rook, was a time-traveling soldier of fortune and Elias illustrated his chronic adventures in an ambitious wash style. In them he got to mix science fiction props, Old West locales, Victorian scenes, and just about everything else he'd drawn in his decades in comics. Since then, Elias has pretty much retired from comics.

Combining Good Girl Art with the Caniff influence. *(Copyright © 1945 Flying Stories, Inc.)*

George Evans

Evans was born in Pennsylvania in 1920. Early interests in aviation and drawing resulted in his selling illustrations to the airplane pulps while still in his teens. He began his comic book career in 1946 at that bastion of Good Girl Art, Fiction House. He'd spent three years in the air force, where "by diligence, application, and KP, he rose to the grade of PFC." Although Fiction House did publish *Wings Comics* and Evans did get to indulge his love for drawing airships in that title, most of his work for them involved more pretty ladies than planes. In his four years there he drew such features as Señorita Rio, Werewolf Hunter, Lost World, Jane Martin, and Tigerman—"My first shot at a really key character in comic books." From Fiction House he moved on to Fawcett, where he drew everything from cowboys to Captain Video.

He joined the EC staff in 1952 and worked on just about every title, doing crime, horror, and science fiction. When EC started its short-lived *Aces High* in 1955, Evans was one of the featured artists, drawing all five covers for the air-minded magazine. Evans also drew for the war-adventure titles edited by Harvey Kurtzman—*Frontline Combat* and *Two-Fisted Tales*. His initial encounter with the dedicated and stubborn Kurtzman didn't exactly inspire him. "The first thing I did for Harvey was the story of Napoleon," he's recalled, "and Harvey wanted me to draw every one of Napoleon's troops, and every one of the Austrians, the Prussians, the Russians and everything else. . . . So I just decided that I didn't have five or six years to put into this, and I did it with variations on his tight layouts. I didn't work for Harvey for a little over a year or so."

Eventually they got together and Evans did some impressive jobs for Kurtzman, but the relationship between them was never a placid one. EC publisher William Gaines has remarked, "Harvey wanted to draw the story himself but knew that George Evans could draw it better. . . . This ended up a Kurtzman story in Evans' style, because Kurtzman really drew the damn thing in his head. . . . Evans hated it. . . . I think Evans deliberately did these things—he made a change that he knew would drive Harvey crazy, he knew that Harvey would not have the nerve to say anything about it, and so it would go through, and then after it was over, Harvey would say, 'You ruined my story.' "

Following the collapse of the EC line, Evans drew for Marvel, Western, and Gilberton's *Classics Illustrated*. On many of the *Classics* assignments he collaborated with Reed Crandall. He once complained, good-naturedly, that Crandall's pencilling "knocked hell out of my carefully laid plans and worked my rump off." Since Gilberton didn't pay much, Evans had calculated that the only way to show a profit was by working fast. When he got Crandall's pages, however, "there in meticulous tight pencilling was the most beautiful comic art I ever saw." Evans says his conscience wouldn't allow him to "ink that kind of stuff with both hands flying."

Nineteen sixty found Evans, anonymously, entering the newspaper strip field. For the next dozen years he provided a good deal of the artwork for *Terry and the Pirates,* improving the look of the strip considerably. Evans also kept drawing for comic books, joining DC in 1968 to draw both humorous and straight stuff. He served a hitch with *Blackhawk* and, of course, did as many air war stories as he could. These last he once described as his "greatest joy." A few years ago, after several stints of ghosting it, he took over the *Secret Agent Corrigan* strip. The daily, begun back in 1934 as *Secret Agent X-9,* has been drawn by a number of notable artists, including Alex Raymond, Austin Briggs, Mel Graff, Bob Lubbers, and Al Williamson. "It no longer pays that much," admits Evans, "but I have been having sheer fun writing and drawing it."

Evans has always been an artist whose strengths aren't of the grandstanding sort. Skillful and efficient, he's turned out a good deal of excellent work over the past four decades. Like a gifted and dependable character actor, though, stardom has eluded him. This probably doesn't bother him too much, however, and he continues to sit down at his drawing board each day with the expectation that he'll have fun at it.

Nobody can draw World War I air combat like Evans. *(Copyright © 1986 William M. Gaines.)*

Bill Everett

Born in 1917, William Blake Everett got into the comic book field when it was nearly brand new. That was in 1938, after a fairly adventurous youth and early manhood that included living on cattle ranches in Arizona and Montana, serving a hitch in the merchant marine, working in the art departments of the Boston *Herald-Traveler* and the New York *Herald Tribune,* and acting as an art director for *Radio News* magazine. In 1939 he created Sub-Mariner, one of the most durable superheroes in comics, and a character Everett was to draw off and on for the rest of his life.

He had a highly individual style, one that blended illustration and cartoon elements. Although he acknowledged the influence of such dissimilar artists as Dean Cornwall, Floyd Davis, and Milton Caniff, you could never mistake his work for that of anyone else. It was compelling, distinctive, and fun to look at. "He was an artist of great facility," Gil Kane has said of him, "but more than that he was an unparalleled storyteller." Everett said of himself, "My education was very limited. I dropped out of high school; I dropped out of art school as well." But he put considerable effort into educating himself. Asked once for his advice on how to succeed as a comic book artist, he replied, "The basic thing is to have the talent to begin with, and to read as prolifically as possible. Read as much of the material that is being produced today, so that you have a basic foundation in it. And then . . . you also *must* have a desire to work and work hard." Everett had the knack of not letting the hard work show in his stuff, which seemed effortless and certain.

His first features were done for the short-lived Centaur line—*Amazing Mystery Funnies, Amazing Man,* etc. He got into the business originally by chance. "I came back to New York to take the world by the heels—and wound up on the unemployment bread line. I was still drawing compensation when I stumbled onto the comic book field." A friend suggested Everett drop in at Centaur, where he did the science fiction strips *Skyrocket Steele* and *Dirk the Demon,* followed by a superhero known as Amazing-Man, who "enjoyed a short but popular life." When Lloyd Jacquet, editor at Centaur, left to start Funnies, Inc., Everett went with him and served as the shop's art director. Funnies, Inc., was a packager, providing art and editorial for comic book publishers. One early customer was Timely (later Marvel) and it was their *Marvel Mystery Comics* that showcased Prince Namor the Sub-Mariner.

Actually Everett's aquatic hero had surfaced initially in a one-shot giveaway called *Motion Picture Funnies Weekly.* Produced by the Jacquet shop, the magazine was a flop. Sub-Mariner fared better in *Marvel,* where his feisty personality and unusual appearance attracted attention from the start. Coming to America from his decimated undersea kingdom, Sub-Mariner was determined to get revenge. "You white devils have persecuted and tormented my people for years," he explained to Betty Dean, the pretty policewoman with whom he carried on a love-hate relationship. Once in Manhattan Namor carried on like an earlier visitor—King Kong. "He was an angry character," reflected Everett much later. "He was probably expressing some of my own personality."

Everett had an affinity for what he called water characters. "I had always been interested in anything nautical, anything to do with the sea—ever since I was born, I guess." For Timely he also created the Fin, for *Heroic Comics* it was Hydroman. This latter character had the dubious ability to change into water. Everett said that when the idea was first suggested to him, "I thought it was utterly preposterous." But he went ahead and did it anyway. His artwork on the early Hydroman stories and on the *Heroic* covers was impressive, compensating for the less-than-inspired concept. Everett also illustrated the debut adventure of Music Master, a fellow with the even-more-dubious ability to change into music, for *Heroic.*

After four years in the army, Everett returned to comics in 1946, "picking up Sub-Mariner where I'd left off." He went on to draw Venus, Namora, and Marvel Boy plus a considerable amount of horror material. Eventually the comic book field experienced one of its slumps —"the whole bunch of us were thrown out on our respective ears, and that was when I decided I'd better find another outlet for whatever talent I might have." Everett found work with various greeting card companies, eventually resettling with his family in his native Massachusetts. Then in 1964 he returned to comic books, once again working for Marvel. He was the original artist on Stan Lee's Daredevil and also worked on the Hulk, Captain America, and Ka-Zar.

Everett was back drawing Sub-Mariner when he died early in 1973. A reformed alcoholic, the last years of his life had contained considerable personal tragedy.

Everett's ultimate aquatic character, a fellow who can actually change into water. (Copyright © 1940 Famous Funnies, Inc.)

Lou Fine

Although he spent nearly three-and-a-half decades as a professional artist, Lou Fine is remembered and revered chiefly for the comic book work he did early in his career. This early work was heroic fantasy material for the most part, drawn in a bravura style that managed to be both forceful and lyrical—a style the restless and commercially oriented Fine tired of after only a few years. Today the Lou Fine of this period is spoken of as "an artist's artist," highly praised by such as Will Eisner, Steranko, and Gil Kane. Since only a portion of the stuff Fine did was signed with his own name, only the more perceptive readers of the time noticed that Louis K. Fine, Kenneth Lewis, Basil Berold, William Erwin Maxwell, and E. Lectron were all one and the same. Interestingly enough, none of the characters he drew during his stint in Golden Age comics, with the exception of the Spirit, came anywhere near being a hit. Almost all of them left comics before he did—proving, perhaps, that excellent artwork is no guarantee of success in comic books.

Born in New York in 1915, Lou Fine studied at the Grand Central Art School and, for a short time, at the Pratt Institute. According to his long-time friend Gill Fox, "as a teen-age boy, Lou's left leg was crippled in one of the polio epidemics that raged in those days. Not being able to participate in sports, he spent his time indoors reading and studying." Among the illustrators he studied were Heinrich Kley, J. C. Leyendecker, and Dean Cornwell. Their influence is noticeable in his comic book pages. Fine signed on in the late 1930s with Eisner and Jerry Iger, to work in their shop and help turn out features for publishers who were jumping into the burgeoning comic book business. "Lou was a very quiet person," Eisner recalls. "He wore steel-rim glasses. Thin nose. Sensitive nostrils. High forehead. Thin. Red hair. Red cheeks. And he had a very shy kind of smile, which at first I thought was just a shy smile. But I found out it was something else. It was a way of showing anger."

Fine's earliest work appeared in the tabloid-sized *Jumbo Comics*—Stuart Taylor, Wilton of the West, The Count of Monte Cristo, etc. His first superhero was the Flame, a fellow who wore a yellow costume with a crimson cape and hood. Fine, who never wrote his own scripts, put considerable enthusiasm into illustrating the Flame's rather prosaic adventures. His pages are full of leaping action and impressive settings, like storyboards for a big-budget, yet simple-minded, movie epic. He also provided numerous covers for *Wonderworld* and its sister publications such as *Mystery Men Comics*. Quite often the package was better than the contents.

Fine's next hero was a teenie weenie one, Dollman, who began his small-scale career in Quality's *Feature Comics* #27 (December, 1939). Fine stuck with the di-minutive do-gooder for less than a year. A much more interesting character, and one Steranko lists among "Fine's most significant triumphs," was drawn for Quality's *Crack Comics*. The Black Condor, originally billed as "the man who can fly like a bird," began his airborne career in the first issue (May, 1940). The most attractive thing about the feature was not the basic concept, not the paranoid plots or the exclamatory dialogue. It was Lou Fine's art. Still under the spell of Leyendecker and Dean Cornwell, he turned out one of the best-looking costumed hero strips of the day. His figure work was exceptional, his settings—whether gloomy Ruritanian castles, Hindustan bazaars, or about-to-be-sabotaged American industrial plants—were always impressive. Fine also seems to have thought about what a man would look like if he actually could fly; his Condor panels are filled with awesome shots of his hero swooping, diving, soaring. Fine, with some help from Charles Sultan and Bob Fujitani, turned out Black Condor episodes for a little over two years.

Smash Comics #14 (September, 1940) introduced the yellow-clad Ray—"transformed by lightning into the powerful combator of crime." His adventures gave Fine the opportunity to draw Gothic castles amply stocked with prowling monsters, haunted mansions, magic kingdoms, and swaggering pirates. Another character Fine did an impressive job on was Uncle Sam, the superpatriotic hero of *National Comics*. The story in #18 is sometimes singled out, not for its exceptional art but for its prophecy. Dated December 1941, that issue of *National* was actually on the newsstands at least a month earlier. In the second panel of the first page we see the Japanese bombing Pearl Harbor.

During the early forties, in addition to all his comic book chores, Fine assisted Eisner on *The Spirit*. When Eisner entered the service in the spring of 1942, Fine took over the drawing of the weekly Spirit stories. Within a year, having abandoned all his flying superheroes, he changed his style drastically. Fantasy and lyricism were gone, replaced by a plainclothes realism. This is some of the least interesting artwork he ever did, but he went on to refine and perfect this approach.

Soon after the end of the Second World War Fine quit comic books and moved into commercial art. In the late 1940s and early 1950s he dominated the Sunday funnies, having as many as a half dozen advertising strips in a single section. This new style was lively, the drawing and layouts highly effective. Fine had arrived at something that was entirely his own. From ad strips he moved on to newspaper strips, drawing *Adam Ames* and later *Peter Scratch*. Neither was a success. At the time of his death, in 1971, he was working on samples of yet another strip.

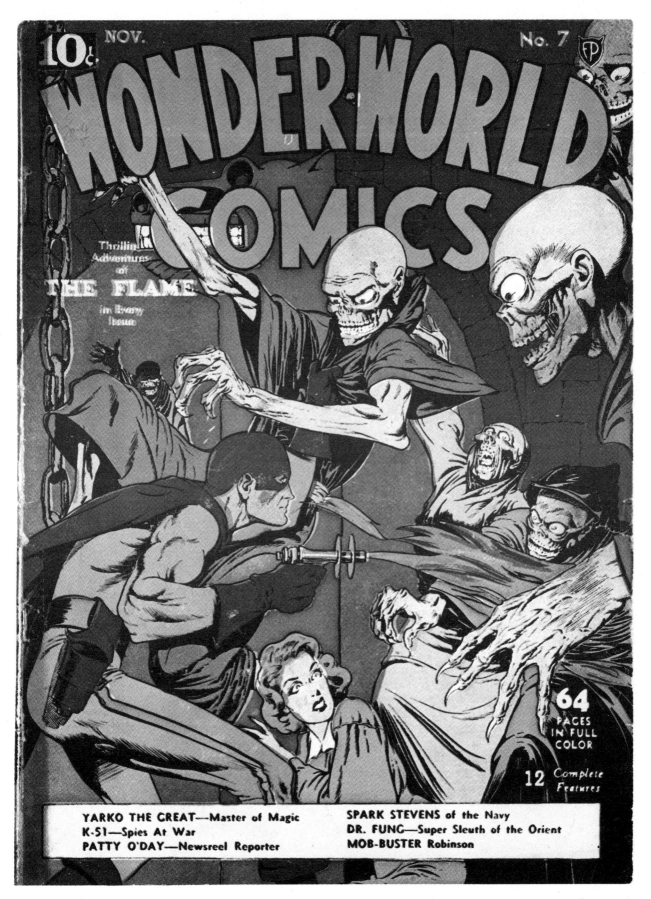

The best thing about many Fox comics of the early 1940s was the Fine cover. *(Copyright © 1940 Fox Publications, Inc.)*

Frank Frazetta

Frazetta spent little more than a decade in comic books and then went on to earn his reputation, along with a substantial income, elsewhere. He managed, though, to attract quite a lot of attention during the relatively few years he was in the field, chiefly with a black-and-white version of the flamboyant fantasy artwork he later did in his full-color cover paintings and posters.

He was born in Brooklyn in 1928. "Began pushing a pencil at age three," he's said. "Attended Brooklyn Academy of Fine Art when eight." While still in his teens he went to work as assistant to John Giunta. The gifted and ill-fated Giunta turned out some exceptional comic book stuff in the middle 1940s, and his influence can be see in Frazetta's rendering and in his early layouts. Another important influence on the young Frazetta was the work of Hal Foster, particularly his *Tarzan* Sunday pages. One of Frazetta's editors supposedly loaned him several *Tarzan* originals to study and this may account for some of the changes evident in his work in the later 1940s.

It was while employed at Bernard Baily's shop that Frazetta's first comic book work started appearing. Next he free-lanced for the Pines titles—*Startling, Thrilling,* etc.—where he drew a variety of features. These included funny animals, teen-agers, and a hillbilly strip called *Louie Lazybones.* For Magazine Enterprises, commencing in 1949, Frazetta turned more serious. He did *Trail Colt, U.S. Marshal* for *Manhunt,* using a loose, Giunta-inspired style. It was with *Ghost Rider* in *Tim Holt* and *Dan Brand* in *The Durango Kid* that he began to do his more ambitious, Foster-influenced drawing. He became more conscious of muscles and weapons, too, and his figures struck more heroic poses. The culmination of this phase came with *Thun'da #1* in 1952. The only complete comic book ever done by Frazetta, it dealt with a bare-chested hero in an Edgar Rice Burroughs lost world setting. In the opinion of *The World Encyclopedia of Comics,* "the book contains four flawlessly drawn jungle tales."

Still in a heroic mood, Frazetta drew *The Shining Knight* and *Tomahawk* for DC. There were also some science fiction and horror jobs for EC. *Famous Funnies* sported a series of his Buck Rogers covers over reprints of the newspaper strip. Frazetta's subsequent reputation has caused these particular issues—numbers 209–216 —to sell for as much as $135 each. Number 208 has a top price of $7.

In 1952 he signed with the McNaught Syndicate to draw *Johnny Comet,* a strip about a racing car driver who was built along the lines of Tarzan. The scripts never matched the art and the strip was garaged after a year. At about this same time Frazetta penciled a four-month sequence of Dan Barry's daily *Flash Gordon.* Subsequently he went to work for Al Capp on *Li'l Abner* and found himself drawing hillbillies again. Frazetta has said he worked for Capp for several years. Capp, who in his last years turned into one of the curmudgeons he used to kid in his strip, maintained Frazetta was only in his employ a matter of months. Apparently the notion that fans would collect *Abner* strips and originals just for the Frazetta touches annoyed him.

Frazetta branched out in the 1960s to do cover paintings, both for magazines like *Creepy* and *Eerie* and for paperbacks. For Ace he did Tarzan and several other Burroughs novel covers. He then painted covers for Lancer's Conan series. These established him as a premier sword-and-sorcery artist and led to a painting career that continues to be increasingly successful. In the early 1980s he teamed up with animator Ralph Bakshi for *Fire and Ice,* a full-length epic that attempted to bring the Frazetta look to the screen. "We co-produced," he said at the time, "and when I say that I mean we co-produced. I did a minimum of drawing, but I did a lot of teaching. I taught the animators how to draw like Frazetta, from the background artists right on down to the figure artists and the colorists." The film was rich with swords, sorcery, brawny barbarians and ample-buttocked maidens—all the Frazetta trademarks—but was not a box-office hit.

Back in 1960, in responding to a National Cartoonists Society questionnaire, Frazetta had listed his hobby as painting and said his ambition was to "someday get just a whiff of the sweet smell of success." It looks like he's gotten his wish.

Proving that Frazetta was equally good with contemporary subjects and didn't need
barbarians and captive maidens to inspire him. *(Copyright © 1986 William M. Gaines.)*

Fred Guardineer

In 1955, at the age of forty-two, Guardineer left comic books and ended a prolific career that had lasted nearly two decades. He was a true nonpareil, an artist whose style was unmistakably his own, and there's been no one remotely like him in the field since.

He graduated from college, with a degree in fine arts, in 1935 and by the following year was in Manhattan laboring in the Harry "A" Chesler shop. His work started showing up in books such as *Star Comics, Funny Pages,* and *Star Ranger.* Guardineer contributed humor fillers, cowboy adventure yarns, sea stories, and illustrations for the text stories. His first continuing feature was *Dan Hastings* in *Star,* a science fiction epic dealing with a future invasion of Earth by aliens. His style was almost fully formed from the start. He seems always to have thought in terms of the entire page, never the individual panel. Each of his pages is a thoughtfully designed whole, giving the impression sometimes that Guardineer is arranging a series of similar snapshots into an attractive overall pattern, a personal design that will both tell the story clearly and be pleasing to the eye. He was another artist who very early understood that a comic book page is not a newspaper page. His drawing style enabled him to create complex pictures by building them up with simple elements. His figures, machines, and buildings have a cartoon look and are rendered in a flat, boldly outlined way. His colors are almost always bright basics. In some ways he was akin to the Chicago school of strip artists—Chester Gould, Harold Gray, etc. In most ways, though, his style was completely unprecedented.

Going out on his own, Guardineer next worked for DC. He drew *Speed Saunders* in *Detective, Anchors Aweigh* in *Adventure,* and *Pep Morgan* and *Zatara* in *Action Comics.* Zatara, a moustached and top-hatted chap who tackled fantastic and supernatural problems that would've given Mandrake the heebie-jeebies, was the first of many magicians Guardineer depicted. In his first two years on the job Zatara met up with the mummy of Cheops; visited Atlantis and battled sea serpents and a giant octopus; encountered, while hunting for a fountain of youth in Brazil, a zombie queen whose throne was surrounded by huge slithering snakes; defeated a hooded villain who had trained giant condors to murder people out on the moors; tangled with another ancient evil queen who exchanged her withered old body for that of a lovely young woman. Although Guardineer later said he would have much preferred doing cowboy strips, he did some of his best work on the odd and mystical adventures of Zatara and such contemporaries as Marvelo, Tor, Merlin, and Mr. Mystic. He also produced quite a few covers for the various DC monthlies, all of them bold and posterlike.

He parted with DC in 1940 to go over to *Big Shot Comics,* where he drew *Tom Kerry, Marvelo,* and *Captain Devildog.* He next did a few jobs for *Silver Streak Comics* and a one-shot for Marvel, then joined the Quality line. There he provided back-up features for several titles: *The Blue Tracer* in *Military, The Mouthpiece* in *Police,* and *The Marksman* in *Smash.* In the immediate postwar years he worked for *Crime Does Not Pay,* drawing both true crime and the magazine's somewhat more cerebral monthly *Who Dunnit* series.

His final go-round was with *The Durango Kid,* a comic book he drew from 1952 to 1955. The backgarbed phantom cowboy was based on the character portrayed by Charles Starrett in B-Westerns, and Guardineer found this one of his most enjoyable jobs. He came to feel, however, that he didn't want to keep working in comic books. "I just had to get out," he once explained, "and set up some kind of security." Leaving the field, he became a postman in his home town on Long Island. He kept up drawing on the side, specializing in hunting and fishing illustrations for local newspapers and specialty magazines. He retired in 1975 and "hung up my mailbag." He's said, "I've enjoyed my lifestyle since then, working on my own time as an artist." He was persuaded to redraw an early *Blue Tracer* episode for the September, 1976, issue of *Cartoonist PROfiles.* That's remained his last comic book work.

Clear-cut, posterlike storytelling in the service of one of FBG's many magical heroes.
(Copyright © 1940 Columbia Comic Corp.)

Paul Gustavson

Gustavson began his comic book career doing humor, but he is best remembered for the flamboyant straight adventure stuff he drew from the late 1930s through the 1940s. He created a troop of second-banana heroes, including the Angel, the Human Bomb, and the Jester.

He was born, as Karl Paul Gustafson, in Finland in 1917, and he and his family moved to the United States in 1921. He went to work as an assistant to gag cartoonist Frank Owen while still in his teens. Owen, who specialized in screwball jokes and had a quirky, eccentric style, may seem an odd mentor for a young man who'd go on to draw superheroes. Gustavson's earliest comic book contributions, though, show an Owen influence and consisted of gag cartoons and humorous filler pages. He made the transition to adventure about the time he left the Chesler shop to go to work for Funnies, Inc., around 1938.

His first attempts in the straight adventure area, which appeared in such Centaur titles as *Amazing Mystery Funnies* and *Funny Pages,* were fairly crude and clumsy. Gradually he improved, his drawing and his storytelling sense growing increasingly better. By the time his moustached superhero the Angel appeared in the first issue of *Marvel Mystery Comics* (November, 1939), Gustavson had nearly arrived at his mature illustrative style.

Nineteen thirty-nine was also the year Gustavson began drawing for the Quality line. It was there that he did his most imaginative and impressive work. For *Crack Comics* he drew Alias the Spider, for *Feature* Rusty Ryan, for *Smash* the Jester, and for *Police* the Human Bomb. He also inherited Quicksilver in *National Comics* and Midnight in *Smash.* He developed, in the early 1940s, a very distinctive style of drawing. Using a fine brush, he worked out an extremely meticulous inking style that used a lot of feathering and shadowing. Equally eye-catching were his layouts. He broke up the pages in unexpected ways, mixing large square panels with small circular ones. At times he'd use as many as a dozen panels on a page, presenting an action sequence in an almost flip-book way. Gustavson's heroes, like those of Jack Kirby, were always on the move and they often burst right out of the bars of the panels.

Unlike his many restless costumed crimefighters, Gustavson was an easygoing man. "Paul was a very relaxed man," his wife has said of him, "with an even-going disposition, and could nap immediately for five to ten minutes any time of day. When he was looking for ideas for his stories, he'd be found on a couch with a pad and pencil on hand. He claimed his best ideas came to him while resting. Then upon rising, he'd draw the characters, in the rough, fill in the balloons as he went along. He wrote most of his scripts until our daughter was seriously injured when hit by a car in 1947; after that only occasionally."

The Midnight character had originally been written and drawn by Jack Cole, a fellow who was able to mix considerable humor with his adventure yarns. Gustavson took over late in 1942 and almost at once his dormant sense of humor was revived. His work became more cartoony, his plots much more whimsical. The Gustavson who'd dreamed up werewolves, zombies, and swamp monsters for do-gooders like the Angel to combat was no more. Turning his back on derring-do, he took up humor again.

When the Second World War ended, comic book publishers found their readers were no longer content with the mixture as before. New types of magazines were tried. Gustavson now drew crime, Western, romance stories. He quit comics in the late 1950s, after a spell of doing funny stuff for the American Comics Group. From then on he worked as a surveyor for the state of New York. He died in the spring of 1977.

A good example of Gustavson's imaginative, restless staging. And yet another of his blonde damsels in distress. *(Copyright © 1941 Timely Comics, Inc. Marvel Comics Group.)*

Bob Kane

Unlike many of his colleagues, Bob Kane's fame rests on just one character—Batman. He created the caped crusader, collaborating with writer Bill Finger, in 1939 and from 1940 until late in the 1960s he was associated solely with him.

Batman made his debut in *Detective Comics #27* (May, 1939). He was on the cover, swinging over the rooftops with an armlock around the throat of a hoodlum in a green pinstripe suit. Inside the magazine the new hero led off the issue in a short, six-page story. Although the pointy ears on his cowl were a little lopsided and his batwing cape didn't fit exactly right, there was something intriguing about him. Once he shaped up and got his act together there was no stopping him. Within less than a year Batman was securely established as one of DC's most popular heroes, second only to Superman. He got his own magazine in the spring of 1940 and by early the following year was also a regular in *World's Finest Comics.* With *Detective #38* he was joined by comics' first boy wonder, Robin.

Kane was born in the Bronx in 1916 and began his professional career twenty years later. He drew a funny filler for the short-lived *Wow!.* The editor there was Jerry Iger, and when the Iger-Eisner shop was formed the following year, Kane was invited to join up. He drew gag cartoons, under such titles as *Jest Laffs,* and a comedy-adventure strip about Peter Pupp. These ran in *Jumbo Comics.* In the Pupp feature, which looks to have been inspired by Floyd Gottfredson's *Mickey Mouse* newspaper strip, Kane first used some of the elements he'd be handling more seriously in *Batman.* Pete was a daring little fellow and a typical four-page sequence had him going up in a fighter plane to combat a giant robot controlled by a satanic villain with one eye in the middle of his forehead.

His first sales to DC were also humorous, one- and two-page comedy stuff. These were *Professor Doolittle,* a pantomime effort for *Adventure Comics; Ginger Snap,* about a wise little girl, for *More Fun;* and *Oscar the Gumshoe* for *Detective.* Kane also began trying his hand at more serious fare. He turned out *Spark Stevens,* about a two-fisted sailor; *Rusty and his Pals,* in the *Terry and the Pirates* vein; and *Clip Carson,* which dealt with a soldier of fortune.

Kane's early work on Batman had a distinctive look. His cartoony style fit the sort of melodramatic, nighttime stories he and Finger loved to spin. "Batman's world took control of the reader," Jules Feiffer has said in *The Great Comic Book Heroes.* "Kane's was an authentic fantasy, a genuine vision, so that however one might nit-pick the components, the end product remained an impregnable whole; gripping and original." The stories, especially during the World War II years, were good, borrowing a little from O. Henry, from Damon Runyon, and from the movies. And, of course, Batman and Robin came up against some of the all-time great comic book villains—the Joker, the Penguin, Catwoman, etc.

"Bill Eisner and I went to DeWitt Clinton High School together," Kane once recalled, "and we were always vying for who would be the top cartoonist." Like Eisner, although on a smaller scale, he set up a shop early on to meet the increasing demand for Batman and Robin material. Finger was the head writer, with teenaged Jerry Robinson the chief assistant. Others who helped out on the artwork were George Roussos, Charlie Paris, and Jack Burnley.

Some of this same crew helped out on the *Batman* newspaper strip that ran, daily and Sunday, from 1943 to 1946. The forties found Batman and Robin as occasional guests on the Superman radio show, and there were two movie serials, neither very compelling, as well. It was in 1966, when the "camp" version of Batman reached TV, that the character made a great leap forward. "Batman became the biggest bit of merchandising the world has seen," Kane has recalled. "That first year —you wouldn't believe it!—they sold over 100 million dollars worth of Batman novelties. It made everybody happy. The public loved the show. It brought money to us."

Kane left comics in the late 1960s, about the same time the *Batman* show left the air. He has also been involved with TV animation—*Courageous Cat, Cool McCool,* etc.—and later tried his hand at gallery painting in the pop art vein. When asked to comment on the lasting popularity of his character, Kane usually professes to have no ready answers. "Who would have dreamed that Batman would go as far as he did?"

The Batman and Robin on a rampage, as depicted by their creator, Bob Kane. *(Copyright © 1940 by DC Comics, Inc.)*

Gil Kane

Kane has been drawing comics for over forty years and talking about them for even longer. Unlike some of his peers, he's an incurable comics fan and is always ready to put forth theories, criticize what he considers inferior work, or just chat about artists whose work he admires. And unlike many critics, he is capable of practicing what he preaches. He's achieved an impressive and effective style by working at it year after year.

He was born in Latvia in 1926. "I was brought up in New York City," he's said. "I grew up feeding my imagination on the inspired work produced by my personal gods of that time—Hal Foster, Alex Raymond, and Milton Caniff." By his middle teens he was employed in the comic book field, free-lancing for MLJ titles and working in the art shops of Jack Binder and then Bernard Baily. He also helped with such Simon and Kirby strips as *Sandman* and *Newsboy Legion*. In addition he drew everything from teen-agers like Candy to costumed crimefighters like the Black Owl. Although he had a great deal of enthusiasm, his drawing at the time was not especially distinguished. Kane feels that while his contemporaries like Alex Toth and Joe Kubert might've been in the boy genius category back then, he himself was not. And he believes that was a good thing. "I think that my triumph was that I was lousy early on," he says, "and it wasn't until I really started to work out systems, to really question the work" that it began to improve.

In 1947 he was hired by editor Sheldon Mayer to draw *Wildcat* for DC's *Sensation Comics*. Kane had been born Eli Katz and hadn't yet decided on what he wanted to call himself. He signed the Wildcat adventures with the name Gil Stack. Within a few more years he'd settled on Gil Kane as a penname and was turning out a great deal of material for DC. Much of it was in the Western genre—*Johnny Thunder, Hopalong Cassidy, The Trigger Twins*, etc.—a category he'd been fond of since discovering the *King of the Royal Mounted* newspaper strip as a boy.

The character that won Kane his first large audience was Green Lantern. A Golden Age retread, the superhero was revived and refurbished by editor Julius Schwartz in 1960. He'd already brought the Flash back to life and felt there was once again a public for superheroes. He picked Kane to do the artwork and had him redesign the born-again hero. Kane's work had improved quite a bit, but what he was doing at that point was just a very slick version of the DC house style of the sixties. The same can be said of his *Atom,* started up two years later.

Kane's real breakthrough came in the middle 1960s, when he did a number of features for Tower's short-lived *Thunder Agents*. He finally arrived at the detailed bravura style he's been building on ever since. "I began to become interested in structure, placement," he says about the changes in his drawing. "Everything that had to do with understanding how things worked and what they looked like underneath. And that for me became a point of view. I worked out of that attitude and I think it's made me what I am today." He went on to say, "In the beginning, what I hated about my work was that it was so timorous. It would just come off in little dribs and drabs, and I could see that it was dominated by one style or influence at this point and another influence at that point. Then I began to make up my mind and come to terms with what I really wanted in the work, and I began to put everything together."

Kane moved over to Marvel in the 1970s to work on Spider-Man, Warlock, Conan, Ka-Zar, etc. He was also their premier cover artist. He returned to DC in the early 1980s and has been drawing the Superman annuals, *Sword of the Atom,* and quite a few covers. Restless and interested in experimenting, he also created a one-shot black-and-white comic called *His Name Is Savage* in 1968. In 1971 he produced a sword-and-sorcery graphic novel, *Blackmark,* for Bantam. He was the artist on the *Star Hawks* comic strip, which began its four-year run in 1977 and was the only double-sized newspaper adventure strip ever. During this period he also drew the *Tarzan* Sunday page.

He recently moved to Southern California and continues to work for DC. It's safe to say he has any number of new projects in mind at the moment. When asked at a comics convention a couple of years ago what he enjoyed drawing, Kane replied, "What I like to draw is some idea of power gathering itself, and all of a sudden that power is blocked and the power has to assert itself and strain itself and there's an enormous resistance to it and all of a sudden the power breaks through and leaps free. That's what I like to draw."

Spider-Man meets the original X-Men, and Gil Kane provides a moody dream sequence.
Script by Gerry Conway, inks by Steve Mitchell. *(Copyright © 1972 Marvel Comics Group.)*

Walt Kelly

Walt Kelly was a contradictory man. In his work he could be gentle and whimsical, while in real life he was often quite the opposite. An expert at drawing lovable animals, pixies, and princesses, he was also an enthusiastic participant in the saloon life of Manhattan. In spite of all the stresses and contradictions, Kelly managed to produce some of the funniest, most visually attractive comic book work of the 1940s. In addition to Pogo, who began life unobtrusively as a comic book character, Kelly drew dozens of other features and turned out hundreds of pages of funny stuff.

Born in 1913 in Philadelphia, Walter Crawford Kelly moved to Bridgeport, Connecticut, two years later along with "father, mother, sister, and sixteen teeth, all my own." The impulse to be a cartoonist hit him quite young and while in high school he drew not only for the school paper and the yearbook, but for the local newspaper as well. Although the majority of his comic book work was produced in the 1940s, Kelly did sell a small amount of work to the magazines in the days before a single superhero had leaped over a single skyscraper.

The turning point of his life, or at least of his drawing style, came when he journeyed to California to work at the Walt Disney studio. While there Kelly "and 1500 other worthies" turned out *Snow White, Fantasia, Pinocchio, Dumbo,* and *The Reluctant Dragon.* Leaving Disney in 1941, he returned to the East Coast. "Back in the U.S.A once more," as he later described his return to the New York area, "Kelly went straight. He got a job doing comic books." He was hired by Oscar Lebeck, who was editing the comics Whitman and Dell were jointly producing and publishing. Fresh from several years of drawing funny animals in Hollywood, Kelly must've seemed ideally suited to go to work on the new kid titles—*Animal Comics, Our Gang,* and *Fairy Tale Parade*—about to be launched.

Kelly split himself in two for comic books. One persona specialized in cute stuff, Disneyized animals and adorable kids. The other, a much more rowdy fellow, had a lowbrow streak mixed in with the cuteness and delighted in slapstick situations and screwball dialogue. The nice Dr. Jeykll side of Kelly's artistic personality is most evident in the sort of work he did for magazines like *Raggedy Ann + Andy, Fairy Tale Parade,* and *Santa Claus Funnies.* For the rag-doll comic he drew a regular feature entitled *Walt Kelly's Animal Mother Goose,* wherein he illustrated nursery rhymes in his best children's-book manner. Although he loosened up a bit when turning *The Gingerbread Man* and similar tales into comic book stories, he was usually careful to remain cute and polite most of the time.

His Mr. Hyde side surfaced in *Pat, Patsy, and Pete,* a screwball saga that starred a pair of real kids, a talking penguin, and a short-tempered pirate named Percy. It appeared, appropriately enough, in *Looney Tunes,* where Kelly drew six episodes in 1943. Moving away from what his predecessors had done and forgetting about fantasy, he turned the feature into a series of slapstick comedies. What Kelly's *Pat, Patsy, and Pete* looks like is a slightly cockeyed version of the Laurel and Hardy shorts, with a touch of the Katzenjammer Kids mixed in for good measure. He was able here to build gags and comedy situations, which he couldn't do in his more sedate stuff. He needed the elbow room and the relative freedom from restraints the monthly eight-page format allowed.

The feature with which Kelly was able to indulge both his cute and rowdy modes began in *Animal Comics* in 1942. Although the original star of the magazine was that venerable rabbit gentleman Uncle Wiggily, Kelly's Pogo and associates eventually pushed him into a second-banana position. Initially Pogo was just a "spear carrier," handicapped, as Kelly later pointed out, "because he looked just like a possum. As time went on, this condition was remedied and Pogo took on a lead role." The feature appeared under a number of titles in its early days—*Bumbazine and the Singing Alligator, Albert and the Noah Count Ark,* etc.—before settling down as *Albert and Pogo.* Bumbazine was a small black boy who shared the swamp with the animals and, in the manner of Christopher Robin, was able to talk to them. As the strip progressed Bumbazine and the other swamp denizens abandoned conventional speech for a patois that was part Southern, part *Li'l Abner*—"Man! Ah di'n't know yo' was a edge-you-cated owl." "Oh, sho! Ah comes from a long line of smart-headed owls."

By the time Pogo reached his cute, nonscraggly state, Bumbazine had departed. The first comic book of nothing but Pogo came along in the spring of 1946, entitled *Albert the Alligator & Pogo Possum.* By 1949 a *Pogo Possum* magazine was being issued on a fairly regular basis. It folded in 1954 after sixteen issues. The Pogo comic strip started running nationally in 1949.

In the comic book Pogo stories, where Kelly had ten or more pages to play around with, he blended smart dialogue and broad comedy situations. The result was something that was both amusing to look at and amusing to read. He couldn't always control his bawdy leanings, and old burlesque routines, including characters dressing up in drag, would now and then show up. At times he'd even slip in the punch line of a well-known dirty joke. What Kelly didn't use in the comic book version of his swamp epic was the political satire, increasingly heavy-handed in his last years, to be found in the newspaper strip. He obviously wasn't taking himself too seriously back then. The result was some of the best-drawn and funniest comic book material produced in the Golden Age.

Kelly turned out hundreds of pages of raffish funny animal stuff. This strip, featuring a derby-wearing mouse named Nibble, ran in *Animal Comics*. (Copyright © 1947 Oskar Lebeck.)

Jack Kirby

Comic books in their present format were only a few years old when Kirby began his career. About half the titles on the stands back then simply reprinted newspaper Sunday pages and strips; many of the others laid out their original material in funny-paper style. Kirby was one of the artists who changed that and gave comic books a vocabulary of their own. He realized early on that he was not telling stories in daily or weekly snippets but in ten- and twelve-page segments that allowed him room to open up. He broke up the pages in new ways and introduced innovative splash panels that stretched across two pages. And he made sure they moved. "I had to compete with the movie camera," he's said. "I felt like John Henry. . . . I tore my characters out of the panels. I made them jump all over the page. I tried to make that cohesive so it would be easier to read."

There was freshness and energy to Kirby's early work. He had a brash, noisy style, that of a tough street kid trying to mask his grace. He was especially good at the figure in action. His characters moved—sometimes the panels couldn't contain them—and when they slugged each other you felt it. His heroes were brawlers, more stuntmen than matinee idols. They didn't care if they mussed their hair and weren't worried about looking handsome in every shot. Kirby's fight scenes blended the violent with the lyrical, a mixture of wrestling and ballet that worked. Somewhat like a choreographed saloon brawl.

His real name is Jacob Kurtzberg and he was born in 1917 on New York's Lower East Side. It was a rough place to grow up and Kirby, a lifelong movie buff, has called it "Edward G. Robinson territory." One of the things the place gave him was "a fierce drive to get out of it." Kirby's earliest escapes were fantasy ones, aided by the movies and the adventure novels—Edgar Rice Burroughs and H. G. Wells were his favorites—he devoured. He was drawing as early as he can remember, and his first published work was for a newspaper put out by a neighborhood club. In 1935 he got a job with the Fleischer animation studios, then located on Broadway in Manhattan. He served as an in-betweener on some of the Popeye shorts. Two years later he went to work for a shoestring syndicate called Lincoln Features. This outfit provided strips and panels to small-town newspapers, and Kirby drew political cartoons, true-fact panels, and an assortment of comic strips for them. Some were drawn in an imitation Alex Raymond manner, others in a rough version of the later Kirby style. To a couple of the features he signed the name Jack Curtiss.

It was as Jack Curtiss, along with two other aliases, that he made his comic book debut. That was in the first issue of *Jumbo Comics,* initially tabloid size, that appeared in the summer of 1938. Kirby was represented by Sunday-page-style features—*Wilton of the West, The Diary of Dr. Hayward, The Count of Monte Cristo.* About this same time, for another small syndicate, he drew a strip called *The Lone Rider.* It was inspired, unofficially, by the *Lone Ranger* radio show and the penname used was the somewhat romantic one of Lance Kirby. By 1940 he was signing his comic book work with a name that borrowed from two of his earlier ones, and he was Jack Kirby from then on.

Although the earliest comic book work was done solo, with Kirby pencilling, inking, and sometimes scripting, his most memorable work in the Golden Age was done in collaboration with Joe Simon. The first Simon and Kirby team-up was for the second-banana superhero Blue Bolt in 1940. They went on to do Marvel Boy, Captain America—one of the most successful comic book characters ever—the Newsboy Legion, the Boy Commandos, Sandman, and Manhunter. The team usually worked with Kirby pencilling and Simon inking, or at least supervising the inking when the work load got too heavy. Simon also handled the business end of things. The work they turned out in the 1940s was impressive. Their Captain America set a style that many subsequent Marvel artists have tried to follow, and their stuff for DC, especially the striking covers for *Adventure* and *Star-Spangled,* boosted sales considerably. After the war they branched out, doing crime books, Westerns, and the first romance comic book. For Harvey they created Stuntman and the Boy Explorers.

In the 1950s Kirby went solo. He, with an assist from Stan Lee, was a major factor in the superhero revival of the 1960s. His work on *The Fantastic Four, Thor, The Avengers,* etc., introduced the mixture of operatic heroics and explosive fantasy that was the foundation of Marvel's immense popularity from the sixties on. When he left Marvel in the early 1970s, he went to DC to draw and write the Fourth World series. This was a complex undertaking, involving such titles as *The New Gods* and *Forever People,* and blending Kirby's bravura drawing with his personal slam-bang cosmology. Since then he's moved around, laboring for a time in animation, drawing alternate press books like *Captain Victory,* and then returning to DC to take another crack at his Fourth World mythology. Although some of the earlier freshness is gone, replaced with the patented Kirby mannerisms, he remains an artist to reckon with.

Captain America plants a Kirby roundhouse right on the Führer's chin. *(Copyright © 1941 by Timely Comics, Inc. and Marvel Comics Group.)*

Bernard Krigstein

A controversial figure in comics, Krigstein's best-remembered and most-argued-about work was done thirty years ago for EC. Although he'd been in the field for several years prior to signing up with the Gaines outfit, drawing such features as *Space Patrol, Nyoka,* and *Wildcat,* Krigstein feels he was restricted as to what he could do in those early years. "EC really provided the atmosphere of freedom and artistic encouragement," he's said. "They allowed me . . . allowed *all* the guys there to develop their own personal ideas."

Krigstein's personal ideas involved the telling of comic book stories in ways that nobody had tried before. "I really feel as if I stumbled upon an important way to tell stories," Krigstein has said, "to break down stories." The breakdown of each page was important to him. To tell the stories in the most effective way possible he abandoned conventional layouts and threw out the splash panel, that traditional teaser that was supposed to lure the reader inside. "I never liked the idea of the splash panel as a storytelling device," he says. "They serve no artistic or dramatic purpose. There's no reason a story can't start right out with the opening situation, instead of having a big panel first."

His approach was thoughtful, each panel making a point, building the mood, moving the story along. Each individual panel was important to him. He also played with time and its often subjective nature. Several events might happen all at once in one large panel. Others might stretch out across a half-dozen small panels—a hunted Nazi war criminal falling from a subway platform, for example. Krigstein was influenced by both the movies and the theater. "Sometimes I'd think in terms of a camera or a movie, and very often I'd think in terms of just a proscenium stage."

Born in Brooklyn in 1919, he entered comics in the 1940s. After service in World War II, he worked for awhile in the shop run by Bernard Baily. He moved on, and "between 1946 and 1949," he says, "I did an enormous amount of work for Fawcett Comics, handling two books: *Nyoka* and *Golden Arrow.*" After that he drew for Timely, Hillman, and Ziff-Davis. It was Harvey Kurtzman who invited him to come to EC, although it turned out that he never did much for the titles Kurtzman edited. Kurtzman has said, in fact, that he "wasn't quite right" for them. Fortunately, EC's other editor, Al Feldstein, liked what he did and publisher Gaines agreed. "Very rebellious and a very fine artist," is how Gaines remembers him. "Strong-willed, serious, a little bit cranky. Basically nice."

The three years he was with EC, Krigstein drew over forty stories—for *Incredible Science Fiction, Crime SuspenStories, The Vault of Horror,* etc. His most widely discussed comic book story was *Master Race,* which appeared in the first issue of EC's *Impact* (March–April, 1955). A simple, grim tale of a chance encounter between two concentration camp survivors —one a former inmate, the other the ex-camp commander—during a ride on a New York City subway, it didn't offer that much new in the way of suspense. The trick of not telling the reader which character was which until the end was not an especially fresh one. But Krigstein took the story, opened it up and applied everything he'd been developing up until then to it. When he was given the story it was to take up just five pages. He felt it needed at least twelve and, after considerable back-and-forth discourse with Gaines, he was allowed to stretch to eight. "It was a masterpiece," Gaines recalls, "but it presented us with a hell of a problem." Because of its new and unexpected length, other stories had to be juggled around.

After a disagreement with Gaines, Krigstein left EC. He continued to work for some of the Atlas titles— *Astonishing, Journey into Mystery, Strange Tales,* etc. —until the late 1950s. Krigstein broke his Atlas stories down into even more panels. The record seems to have been reached in the April, 1956, issue of *Uncanny Tales* with a tale entitled *They Went Below,* in which he fit seventy-five panels into just four pages. Even when using as many as twenty panels on a page he almost never lost clarity or gave the impression of clutter. "Those were the last things I did," Krigstein explains. "I was really writing messages and sending them to sea in a bottle there. Those stories were my attempt at carrying out an object lesson of how comic book stories could be broken down . . . to show the limitless ways that a comic story could be unfolded."

The CATACOMBS

PIETRO MIUTA...

...GRABBED THE SACK WITH ITS LOAD OF SILVER...

...AND, WITH GINO ALCARI FOLLOWING...

...BROKE FOR THE FRONT DOOR!

AS THE FRIGHTENED PAIR FLED DOWN THE STREET, THE STARTLED CRIES OF THE ROBBED OLD MAN SHAT- TERED THE STILLNESS, THEN DRIFTED OFF INTO THE SILENT DARKNESS...

Krigstein's stop-time breakdowns in action. *(Copyright © 1986 William M. Gaines.)*

Joe Kubert

One of the comic book field's child prodigies, Kubert began working professionally while in his early teens. He started in the late 1930s as a sort of apprentice at the art shop run by the enterprising Harry "A" Chesler. By the time he was sixteen he was doing back-up features in *Police Comics, Speed Comics, Smash Comics,* and several other magazines. In addition to his own stuff, Kubert inked the work of such substantial artists as Lou Fine, Mort Meskin, and Jack Kirby, and he credits this as an important part of his education. He came to the attention of editor Sheldon Mayer and in 1944 was assigned his first major character, Hawkman in *Flash Comics.* He was responsible for nearly three dozen Hawkman stories and contributed sixteen covers to *Flash.* During his initial stint with DC, Kubert also drew the Flash, Dr. Fate, and Sargon the Sorcerer.

His drawing in the 1940s has a highly individual look. He had a lush inking style, rich with feathering and shadows. Although his figure work was not exactly perfect, Kubert's staging and his depiction of action were impressive. He was very good at creating the mood of fantasy required in Hawkman, Sargon, and the assorted weird tales he illustrated for comics like Avon's *Eerie, The Challenger*—where one of his stories was a handsome seventeen-page adaption of the Golem legend—*All New, Planet Comics,* etc. Kubert doesn't think highly of much of what he did in this period. "Looking at some of that material," he says, "at the distortions and bad drawing, gives me the shudders." He is, of course, comparing the youthful Kubert with the much more slick and professional Kubert of today. To many readers of the forties, though—myself included—his work stood out as being exceptionally attractive.

The World Encyclopedia of Comics is fonder of the Kubert of the 1950s. "Perhaps Kubert's finest work," they say, "came during the 1950–1955 period when he was an editor on a short-lived prehistoric strip called *Tor.*" The *Tor* comic book is also one of Kubert's favorites. "It was conceived while I was in the army in 1950, on a troopship heading for Germany. I still have the notes and sketches I did at the time." The 1950s saw him, out of the service and abandoning DC for awhile, drawing for a variety of other publishers. During this decade he turned out Westerns, horror, comedy, romance, and science fiction. He even did a few jobs for EC's *Frontline Combat* and *Two-Fisted Tales.*

"At one time or other," he's said, "I've worked for possibly every comic book publishing house in the business."

Kubert returned to DC in the 1960s and has been there ever since. He drew Hawkman once again when the superhero boom caused the winged crimefighter to be revived. There was a swing away from fantasy in these years and he began to do a great deal of realistic combat stuff, notably with the World War II hero Sgt. Rock in *Our Army At War* and the World War I German aviator Enemy Ace in *Star-Spangled War Stories.* When DC acquired the rights to Tarzan in 1972, Kubert was selected to be the artist. He said at the time that he went back to the Sunday pages of the thirties. "I've tried to pore over Hal Foster's old Tarzan work and to get out of it that feeling of excitement it generated in me when I first saw it years ago. I'm trying to accomplish a simplification of my illustrations, and I want to hit home on the vibrant points of telling the story—concentrating on these rather than making too florid an illustration. I'd like to keep the drawings as direct, as effective, and as strong as I can."

In recent years he's concentrated more on editing and on running the Joe Kubert School of Cartoon and Graphic Art, Inc., in New Jersey. He does very effective and imaginative covers for many DC titles and still finds time for an occasional story. There are many who consider him one of the best graphic storytellers going. Writing in *The Comics Journal,* critic R. C. Harvey has said, "The essential quality in Kubert's storytelling is contrast. He contrasts the large and the small, with inset panels imbedded in splash panels, with long shots and close-ups, and with rapidly shifting camera angles. Other cartoonists do this, too, of course. But the contrasts appear more vivid, more jolting in Kubert's work because his drawings are relatively simple."

Kubert's move into newspaper strips was made with *Tales of the Green Beret.* This was in 1966, when a great many people weren't in the mood to take a comic strip about war in Vietnam to their hearts. Kubert abandoned it the following year. He put in a brief spell in 1981 drawing the *Winnie Winkle* strip, and he was mentioned as the artist to do a proposed revival of *Terry and the Pirates,* but nothing came of the latter project. All in all, he never came near equalling his comic book success in newspapers.

Kubert was doing impressive work even early in his career. *(Copyright © 1946 Interfaith Publications.)*

Harvey Kurtzman

He's been called one of the three greatest American comic book artists—Barks and Eisner were the other two. *The Comics Journal,* which nominated him for that triumvirate, applauded Kurtzman for "the originality and uncommon intelligence of his approach to the comics medium" and for his "bold, expressionistic style, which no one has ever matched." Interestingly enough, almost all of the work that's earned Kurtzman his accolades was done in the single decade following the end of World War II.

Born in New York in the autumn of 1924, Kurtzman was working in comic books before he was out of his teens. His first job was in a shop run by Louis Ferstadt, a leftist painter who earned his living producing features for DC, Timely, Ace, etc. Kurtzman drew such second-banana superheroes as Magno and Lash Lightning for various Ace titles and did some humor fillers on his own for *Police Comics,* etc. None of this stuff, which consisted of conventional "bigfoot" art, was in the style now associated with him.

After getting out of the service in 1945, "I got together with Willie Elder and a guy named Charlie Stern. We were going to be a commercial art studio. First we got ourselves a skylit loft and then we moved to a second-story storefront. We called it the Charles William Harvey Studio, and a lot of interesting people ran in and out."

While part of the studio, Kurtzman did some of his earliest work in his distinctive humorous style. First came a series of one-page fillers, called *Hey Look!,* for various Marvel titles. Drawn in a loose, thick-outlined way and often reversing black and white and looking like negatives, these were wild and violent things. Explosions, fires, people eating furniture, axes, and machine guns were frequently to be encountered. Many of the *Hey Look!* pages remind you of storyboards for animated cartoons, ones that even an avant-garde studio like UPA would've found too strange to touch. Working in a similar vein, he did *Silver Linings* for the New York *Herald Tribune.* Although drawn in a daily strip format, it ran in color in Sunday funnies sections around the country. For *John Wayne Comics,* of all places, he turned out five-page cowboy parodies starring Pot-Shot Pete, the sheriff of Yucca-Pucca Gulch.

Kurtzman first got together with William Gaines and EC in 1950. Initially he had approached them about doing nonfiction-type comics—"One thing I was working on, I was trying to explain the ulcer graphically." He also included samples of *Hey Look!* in his portfolio and these impressed Gaines and editor Al Feldstein even more than the ulcer. "We were just dying," Gaines has recalled, "our stomachs ached with laughter." In spite of that, the first job Kurtzman did for EC was a straight educational comic booklet on syphilis titled *Lucky Fights It Through.* Work for the horror and science fiction titles followed.

Next came *Two-Fisted Tales* and *Frontline Combat,* which Kurtzman edited as well as drew for. He's said, "All our stories really protested war. I don't think we thought war was very nice generally." Everything in these war magazines was exhaustively researched and Kurtzman's own stories had a stark, grim look. His straight drawing was unconventional, a bit cartoony, and boldly inked.

Nineteen fifty-two was the year Kurtzman came up with his major contribution to comics. "I'd always been doing satire in school, in the streets; it was my kind of clowning," he says. "When I wanted to win popularity, I'd draw a cartoon. . . . So I proposed the format *Mad,* I proposed the title, made little title sketches and showed it to Gaines, and he said, 'Go ahead!' The format would make fun of comic books as they were at that particular period. So I had a 'horror' story and a 'science fiction' story and so forth. We used the physical format of EC —four stories, with the legal text requirement in the center. I gathered in my favorite artists, I wrote the stories, laid them out, and that is the God's honest truth on how *Mad* started."

A success almost from the start, *Mad* is still with us. Kurtzman, for various reasons, left the fold soon after *Mad* switched from comic book to magazine format in 1955. He went on to edit and contribute to *Trump, Humbug,* and *Help!* None of them thrived. He began drawing and writing, with considerable help from his friends, the *Little Annie Fanny* strip in *Playboy* in the early 1960s, and is still at it. Asked once for his opinion of his own work, Kurtzman replied, "I have a high opinion of my work. And at the same time a low opinion. I really like my stuff, but I'm very dissatisfied with it in the sense that I wish it could be a lot better. I think my stuff is great, but I'm completely convinced that I'm the only one who thinks so." His modesty hasn't prevented him from coming up with new projects. Most recently he's edited *Nuts!,* a humor magazine in paperback format. He's also back contributing ideas to *Mad.*

Proof positive that there's only one Kurtzman. *(Copyright © 1986 Harvey Kurtzman.)*

Joe Maneely

If you look only at the statistics, you might conclude that Maneely was nothing more than a very prolific hack. In the ten years he worked in comic books he turned out dozens of features and drew nearly six hundred covers for Marvel alone. When you look at his pages, though, you see that he was a gifted man with an effective and individual style. Fast he was, but also, almost always, good.

Pennsylvania-born, he studied at Philadelphia's Hussian School of Art and later worked on that city's *Daily News.* He did his first comic book work in 1948, when he was twenty-two. That was for such Street & Smith titles as *Super Magician Comics, Red Dragon,* and *The Shadow.* It's probable that this earliest material was done for an art shop in the Philadelphia area that was fronted by William de Grouchy, who was also editing the S&S comics line.

While there Maneely drew Nick Carter, miscellaneous historical fillers, the Red Dragon, and Tao Anwar. Both the unusually named Tao Anwar and the Red Dragon were magicians. Tao, a full-grown young man billed as a "Boy Magician," was simply a stage illusionist who dabbled in amateur detection. RD possessed real magic powers and, accompanied by a Chinese sidekick and a Komodo dragon lizard, tangled with all sorts of mystical threats in a variety of oriental settings. At about the time Maneely commenced his Street & Smith career, the exceptional pulp illustrator Edd Cartier—who did first-rate work in *The Shadow, Doc Savage, Unknown,* and *Astounding*—had a brief fling in some of the same comic books. Maneely seems to have been influenced by the older artist, particularly in his inking and in his slightly less than serious approach to depicting adventure and fantasy.

Maneely began his association with Marvel in the late 1940s and eventually moved to the New York area. Throughout most of the 1950s he was one of the stars of the Marvel bullpen. Since the fifties was not a decade in which superheroes thrived, Maneely was kept busy drawing in the dozens of other categories Marvel hoped would sell instead. These included horror, Western, science fiction, jungle, war, crime, historical, romance, and funny animal. He also contributed to *Riot* and *Wild,* short-lived imitations of *Mad.*

In the middle 1950s, when some of the older Marvel heroes made a not-too-successful try at a comeback, Maneely drew covers for such titles as *Sub-Mariner.* He turned out, as mentioned above, hundreds of covers in the fifties. His design sense was strong, his figure work good, and he'd developed a distinctive style of inking— one utilizing considerably quirky feathering. Marvel often used his striking covers to package interior art by others that was only a few staggering steps from passable.

Westerns were one of his strong suits and he did a great many—*Kid Colt, Apache Kid, Whip Wilson, Wyatt Earp* and, possibly his best one, *The Ringo Kid.* His approach was both gritty and romantic, similar to that of the later Spaghetti Westerns. While seeing to it that the cowboy heroes were acceptably handsome and rough-hewn, he also paid attention to his villains, sidekicks, and bit players. They were rarely stock figures and were always well defined individuals.

His *Black Knight,* a medieval epic that appeared briefly in the middle 1950s, was also impressive. Robert Jennings, a comics historian, has said of Maneely that "he surpassed all his previous work with the Black Knight. The historical background was rendered up with fine line detail and a careful attention to accuracy. Romantic realism is perhaps the best way to describe it."

In addition to all his chores for Marvel, he found time to do several careful and impressive jobs for DC's crime and fantasy titles. He also drew a humorous Sunday page, with script by Stan Lee. *Mrs. Lyons' Cubs,* dealing with a den mother and her charges, was syndicated by Field Enterprises.

Maneely was killed in 1958 in a fall from a car of the Long Island Railroad. He was just thirty-two years old.

Maneely in his dependable science fiction mode. *(Copyright © 1953 Cornell Publishing Corp. and Marvel Comics Group.)*

Jesse Marsh

Neither fame nor fortune ever touched him. He spent over twenty years in comic books, drawing some of the best-known characters, real and fictional, in the world—Tarzan, Gene Autry, Davy Crockett—and managed to remain virtually unknown. Marsh died two decades ago, and in the intervening years little attention has been paid to the enormous amount of work that he produced. He was, however, a very gifted and highly individual artist. His qualities, for the most part, were more appreciated by his employers and some of his colleagues than by the average reader. Fellow *Tarzan* artist Russ Manning was a great champion of Marsh's work. He described it, some years after Marsh's death, as "original, unique, resolutely noncommercial, non-'comic book,' finely designed." Manning also said, "The best of his work appeals today only to those able to appreciate cultures other than that of comic books."

Marsh lived in Southern California and all his comic book work was done for the Dell-Western offices there. He moved into comics while still employed as a story man at the Walt Disney Studios. He'd gone to work for Disney in 1939, when he was in his early thirties, and was one of the many contributors to such full-length animated features as *Fantasia, Pinocchio,* and *Make Mine Music.* His first job in comics was drawing Gene Autry, initially for a series of one-shots about the popular singing cowboy and then in the regularly issued title that commenced in 1946. Alex Toth, another long-time Marsh admirer, discovered him about this time and was immediately impressed by his "rather low-key style of storytelling—so far afield from the wild and woolly New York City-based artwork. . . . I realized Jesse was one to watch."

In 1946 Dell decided to try a *Tarzan* comic book that would offer brand new material instead of the newspaper reprints issued by previous publishers. Marsh was chosen to be the artist. It was an unconventional choice, since up until this time Tarzan had almost always been drawn in the heroic, larger-than-life manner established by Hal Foster and carried on and inflated by Burne Hogarth. True, Rex Maxon hadn't exactly followed their path on the daily strip, but Edgar Rice Burroughs loathed his work and had been urging the newspaper

syndicate to dump him for years. Although a considerably better artist than Maxon, Marsh was certainly not in the Foster-Hogarth camp. He was much closer to the lushly inked realistic style favored by Caniff and Noel Sickles. He proceeded to draw a book-length *Tarzan* adventure that was unlike anything seen before by jungleman buffs. A second book didn't follow until the next year, but sales must eventually have been satisfactory, because early in 1948 a bimonthly was launched. Marsh was the artist, and he remained with the magazine for over 150 issues. "It was *Tarzan* that opened up his talents and my eyes," Toth has said. "New broad picture-making vistas, encompassing the whole of Africa and its peoples, tribes, costumes, customs, terrain, and wildlife, put him on the map for me. It was a delight to see him grow, with the series established as a hit—each issue was a surprise."

One of the areas where Marsh excelled was in his settings—the jungles, forests, veldts, the lost cities, the hidden valleys where prehistoric monsters still roamed. His Africa wasn't the fantasy land of the Sunday pages and the movies, but a real place, albeit rich with romance and mystery. Nobody drew blacks as well as Marsh or with such an eye for variety and individuality, and his women were distinctive and real. He had the ability, somewhat rare in comic book artists, to draw the figure at ease or performing simple everyday actions. His Jane was especially fine, not only fighting side by side with her mate against the latest threat to the peace of the jungle, but preparing a meal, spearfishing, or simply sitting in a woodland clearing. The character that gave him the most trouble was Tarzan himself. Toth has commented on the problems Marsh had with the jungle lord's anatomy and said, "Tarzan was, it seems, a chore for him."

Marsh produced a great many other comics. There were Westerns—*Roy Rogers, Rex Allen, Annie Oakley*—movie adaptations, and even Burroughs's *John Carter of Mars.* He worked very fast, which explains how he was able to produce a Sunday page based on the current Disney movies—*Robin Hood, Swiss Family Robinson, Rob Roy,* etc.—for many years along with his comic book output. He retired in 1965 to devote his time to painting. He died the following year.

An example of Marsh's way with figures and foliage. (Copyright © 1959 Edgar Rice Burroughs, Inc. All rights reserved.)

Sheldon Mayer

While the majority of boys growing up in the late 1930s and early 1940s no doubt wanted to be stunt pilots, baseball stars, movie cowboys, and swing musicians when they reached the adult state, there must have been a small multitude who yearned to be professional cartoonists. Several comic books of the period acknowledged this dedicated minority. *Tip Top Comics,* for instance, provided two pages each issue where amateurs, after competing with the frenzied enthusiasm of gladiators, might see their work in print. Other magazines offered similar contests, cartoon tips, and drawing lessons.

But best of all there was *Scribbly.* Scribbly was a boy cartoonist created by Mayer when he was nineteen and still a boy cartoonist himself. The feature began in the second issue of *The Funnies* (November, 1936). The magazine, along with *Popular Comics* and later *The Comics,* was a sixty-four-page compilation of newspaper strip reprints that M. C. Gaines was producing to cash in on the just-commencing comic book boom. "I went to work for M. C. Gaines in January of 1936," Mayer recalls. "I had been up to see him the previous summer and half a year later he gave me a call and offered me a few days of paste-up work. I started pasting up newspaper strips in comic book format." His *Scribbly* pages were laid out like Sunday pages, each with its own logo. Mayer did this so his upstart filler could rub shoulders undetected with the real Sunday pages.

"*Scribbly* was a thing I dreamed up during my lunch hour one day in a noisy cafeteria," Mayer has said. "I followed the old rule of writing only about what you know. What was more natural than writing about the adventures of a boy cartoonist?" Mayer had dreamed of being a professional cartoonist for as long as he could remember, and he wasn't going to content himself with the recycling of other people's strips.

The feature was drawn in a style that was appealing, exuberant and, you might say, scribbly. The saga dealt with Scribbly Jibbet, who was young, diminutive, bespectacled, and possessed of a head of hair like an untidy haystack. He was intent on breaking free of the bonds put upon him by home, school, and contemporaries and entering into that charmed world of newspaper cartooning. Mayer has said that the strip was a blend of autobiography and fantasy and that some of the truest-seeming elements are the most unreal. The urban area Scribbly inhabited was a somewhat sanitized version of the one Mayer grew up in. "East Harlem . . . was a rough, tough neighborhood in those days. Kids began to think about what they were going to do for a living from the day they were born, because everybody wanted to get out of there as soon as possible."

Scribbly next showed up in *All-American Comics,* one of a string of titles Gaines and Mayer put together for DC. In the real world, meanwhile, Mayer was knee deep in supermen—Green Lantern, the Flash, Hawkman, and the entire Justice Society. He needed a place to comment on some of the sillier aspects of the super life and decided the place to do that was in his own *Scribbly* pages. Thus the Red Tornado was born. One of the few female costumed heroes of the day, she soon came to dominate the strip. Any heroine who wore red flannels, bedroom slippers, and an inverted stew pot for a mask was bound to attract attention.

Mayer abandoned *Scribbly* in the middle 1940s to concentrate on editing. He did some drawing for *Funny Stuff,* turning out the fifth issue of the funny animal title entirely on his own. After stepping down as a DC editor, he drew all sorts of funny animal strips—*Bo Bunny, Doodles Duck, The Three Mousketeers,* etc. His other major creation came along in 1956. *Sugar & Spike* was unlike other kid comics. Its two toddler stars weren't even able to talk yet, or so the unimaginative adults around them thought. Actually they communicated quite well with each other. This helped them get through the wild and fantastic adventures they had. Mayer had enormous fun with the nearly 100 issues of this book he wrote and drew, alternating simple everyday continuities with slapstick and complex fantasy. "His style was always so intensely personal to these characters," writer Mark Evanier has said, "that they wouldn't be themselves in any other motif. No artist ever seemed more indispensible to his features than Sheldon Mayer."

In recent years, after some time off because of eye trouble, Mayer has been drawing again. He produced new *Sugar & Spike* material for overseas markets and did covers for digest reprints of their adventures in this country. It's possible he'll be reviving them again soon.

From an episode of *J. Worthington Blimp, Esq* that ran, unbeknownst to Mayer, in *Funny Pages.* (Copyright © 1936 Comics Magazine Company, Inc.)

Mort Meskin

Beyond a doubt Meskin is one of the most gifted and least appreciated cartoonists ever to work in comics. An artist's artist, highly thought of by such colleagues as Gil Kane, Alex Toth, and Jerry Robinson, he never managed to excite the sort of mass audience needed to guarantee stardom.

There are perhaps several reasons for this. Meskin was a subtler, less flamboyant artist than some of his contemporaries. And it was his fate never to be assigned the front-running heroes. While others in the 1940s were gaining attention with Batman, Green Lantern, and the Flash, he had to be content with back-up characters like Johnny Quick, Vigilante, and Starman. Basically shy, he seems content to let his work speak for itself and has never attended a comics convention or participated in a panel discussion. He doesn't even enjoy being interviewed and will only talk to interviewers over the phone, never face to face. As a result little has been written about him in the burgeoning fan press in the years since he left comics for the better-paying field of advertising. The Overstreet *Comic Book Price Guide* does include him among the eighty or so "better artists" whose work is pointed out in the listing of comic book titles, but he is one of those who gets a nod only for his "most noted work" and not his entire output.

Morton Meskin was born in Brooklyn in 1916 and got his basic art training at the Pratt Institute and the Art Students League. Equally important to his education were newspaper comics—Alex Raymond and Milton Caniff were his favorites—and pulp magazines. He's said he was much influenced by two of the most talented pulp illustrators of the thirties and forties, Edd Cartier and Herbert Morton Stoops. Cartier did a considerable amount of fantasy and science fiction illustration for *Unknown* and *Astounding,* but what Meskin liked best were the graceful, impressionistic drawings he did in *The Shadow* in the 1930s. Stoops was the premier illustrator in *Blue Book,* an adventure pulp that attracted a great many excellent artists. His black-and-white interior work, with impressive figure work, layouts, and lighting, made a strong and lasting impression on Meskin.

Though Meskin women are usually slim and realistically built, his first comic book job was illustrating the cliff-hanging adventures of the jungle amazon Sheena in *Jumbo Comics.* He did that in 1938, while working in the Eisner-Iger shop. By the time he went to work for MLJ in 1940, his style had improved greatly. A thoughtful artist, he gave considerable attention to how best to stage the less-than-brilliant scripts he was called upon to illustrate for *Zip Comics, Pep Comics, Blue Ribbon,* etc. His shots were carefully selected to keep the action flowing and it should come as no surprise that after leaving comics he went to an advertising agency to do storyboards. There's a freshness to his MLJ pages; they convey his enthusiasm and are full of surprising and unconventional graphics. He took care of costumed crimefighters, detectives, jungle boys, and soldiers of fortune. The closest thing to a top banana was the Wizard, MLJ's moustached answer to Superman.

He left MLJ, the future home of Archie, in 1941 and went to DC for a long stay. This was the comic book equivalent of switching from the Republic studios to MGM. His earliest assignment was *Vigilante,* a feature he drew from its debut in *Action #42* late in 1941 through the autumn of 1946. The character, an urban cowboy fighting crime, apparently inspired Meskin. His drawing got even better—although, for some reason, he had a difficult time getting his hero's Stetson to sit straight on his head in the early episodes—and he began constructing splash panels that rivalled anything Simon and Kirby were doing. "Mort took what might otherwise have been just another middle-class hero series and transformed it into a strip of terrific visual literacy," says Jim Steranko in his *History of the Comics,* "one with genuine vitality and crackle. . . . He experimented, developed a new set of comic book tricks, and deplored the use of 'stock shots.'" Meskin was equally inventive with Johnny Quick, "the King of Speed," in *More Fun Comics* and with Wildcat in *Sensation.*

Leaving DC for a spell, he teamed up with Jerry Robinson to do the Black Terror and the Fighting Yank for the Ned Pines line. These two lackluster heroes never looked so good. In the fifties and sixties, like many others, Meskin drew crime, romance, science fiction, and horror. There are fine stories from these years, but some of the work looks hurried and dispirited. While even a less-than-inspired Meskin page is better than most, much of his later work simply doesn't match what he was doing in the forties. He left comics for good two decades ago and went into advertising.

An impressive piece of teamwork, with Meskin pencilling and Jerry Robinson inking.
(Copyright © 1948 Visual Editions, Inc.)

Frank Miller

Frank Miller has been a popular name for cartoonists. There was the Frank Miller who drew the *Barney Baxter* newspaper strip and Frank Miller of the Des Moines *Register* who won a Pulitzer Prize for his political cartoons. Our Frank Miller was born in 1957, long after the Golden Age had ended, and is one of the more innovative and/or controversial storytellers of the 1980s.

He began his professional career at age twenty, moving up from fanzine work. "I was born in Maryland. My parents moved to Vermont when I was a very small child," he has said. "I lived there until I was twenty." His fascination with comics commenced early on. "I grew up as a comic book junkie," Miller admits. "I think that came from being miserable in Vermont, from being a maladjusted child." As for his art background, he says, "I've had classes in art, but I've not had formal, regimented training. I've probably learned most of what I know about drawing from reading and from working in the field."

His first published work appeared in the *Twilight Zone* comic book in 1977. But it was with long-time superhero Daredevil, which he took over in the spring of 1979, that Miller began to attract attention, praise and some violent critical reaction. Marvel got things rolling by introducing him with the modest statement, "From time to time a truly great new artist will explode upon the Marvel scene like a bombshell."

Miller seems to have built his personal style from a wide range of sources—Eisner, Japanese prints, Bernard Krigstein, martial arts movies, and European artists like Moebius and Guido Crepax. He has been always very much aware that page breakdowns can be used to control and manipulate time. Like Krigstein at EC in the 1950s, Miller has experimented with multipaneled pages. He's sliced them up vertically, horizontally, sometimes cut a tier in to a half-dozen or so frames. Every decade or so a few young artists will come along and reexamine the established ways of telling a story. Miller is one of those.

His *Daredevil,* and especially the character Elektra, aroused all sorts of emotions among readers and reviewers. The violence and the thoughtful layouts, which sometimes looked too calculated and showboating, all touched off responses. These ranged from "Miller's comics are the greatest comics that have been done in the history of mankind" to "At best, modestly entertaining work." As he continued with the book he garnered more praise—"Miller skillfully exploits the medium"; scholarly hysteria—"Neo-Eisnerian cinematics and panelogical underscorings"; and further attacks—"[Not] an interpretation of life or an imaginative counterpoint to life, but an interpretation of various forms of pop culture *kitsch.*"

Undaunted, Miller continued. His 1982 *Wolverine* stirred up more controversy, as did his *Ronin* miniseries done for DC in the following year. Of this latter book, Miller says, "I had a wonderful feeling of freedom doing *Ronin.* Now I feel my stories can come from everything I read, everything I see, and everything I've lived through."

Most recently he has returned to *Daredevil* as writer, and done an *Elektra* graphic novel and a special *Batman* miniseries. With the venerable caped crusader Miller wanted to get back to basics. "I see Batman as a quasi-mystical character," he explains. "He's also unrelentingly righteous. He's someone who, when he was very young, had his entire world demolished so that it no longer made sense. Now he's forcing the world to make sense. . . . Superhero comics have forgotten what they are. They've become so built on their own padding that people have forgotten the basic appeal and the basic purpose of these characters." These works show Miller continuing to experiment with new layouts and new ways of telling his stories. "If the comic is just a weakened, watered-down version of someone else's vision, if it's a remake of something old," he feels, "you're not going to get the emotion or the value. That's why it's important that a lot more experimental and radical work happen. Things have got to bust open."

A sample of Miller's cinematic style featuring Elektra, his most popular character. *(Copyright © 1981 Marvel Comics Group.)*

Bob Montana

Montana is remembered for just one creation: that improbable and perennial teenager, Archie Andrews. In the early 1940s, though, before the redheaded Archie came to dominate his life, he was a prolific and versatile comic book artist. In those days Montana applied his four-square, uncluttered style to superheroes, detectives, crimebusters, and even other teenagers.

He was born in 1920 in Stockton, California, into a show business family. He once said he was "raised in vaudeville" and "did rope tricks in Pop's Western act." The habit of traveling that he picked up in his youth stuck with him all his life. He studied art in Arizona, Boston, and New York, and by the time he was twenty-one he was settled in Manhattan and working as a professional cartoonist.

According to Montana, his first job was as assistant to Bob Wood, who drew the Target and Silver Streak before coediting *Crime Does Not Pay.* He began soloing for the MLJ line in 1941, drawing such second-banana characters as the Fox, Inspector Bentley, and Danny in Wonderland. For the Victor Fox outfit he worked, anonymously, on Spark Stevens, Lu-Nar, and other unmemorable characters. Montana also contributed quite a few covers to MLJ during the early years of World War II. His intricate covers, rich with voluptuous women in jeopardy, Nazi fiends, slavering Japanese, machine guns, knives, branding irons, and brightly costumed superheroes making hairbreadth rescues, graced *Zip, Top-Notch, Jackpot,* and *Pep.*

Archie himself arrived on the scene late in 1941, showing up just about simultaneously in *Pep* #22 and *Jackpot* #4. The first splash panel in *Pep* showed Archie and Betty barreling along in a red rattletrap of a car. "Hang onto your hats, Riverdale," warned the first caption. "Here comes ARCHIE with his first jumpin' jivin' jallopy! Betty Cooper says everything makes noise but the horn . . . and right now she's finding out that the roughest distance between two points is a ride with . . . ARCHIE!" Archie's plump businessman dad was in the story, too, along with his understanding mom. But not Jughead, who made his debut over in *Jackpot.* The dark-haired Veronica came slinking into Archie's life a few months later.

Montana used an attractive, animated style on Archie, favoring crosshatching and other pen techniques that had been the staple of cartoon courses for years. Most of the plots were pure sitcom, with some slapstick thrown in—comic book versions of the sort of thing Henry Aldrich was up to on the radio. The Archie version of teen life was one a great many readers took to and his star began to rise. The first issue of his own magazine came out in the fall of 1942 and by late 1947 he'd nudged all the serious heroes out of *Pep* and was its uncontested leading man. Eventually the MLJ company changed its name to Archie.

During his early years with Archie, in between drawing jalopies, jukeboxes, and jitterbugs, Montana found time to do some work for his old mentor Bob Wood. For the Gleason line, edited by Wood and Charles Biro, he did *Dickie Dean,* dealing with a boy inventor, and *Whirlwind,* about a boxer. He also managed to turn out a few gruesome jobs for the initial issues of *Crime Does Not Pay.* Montana left comic books to enter the service and spent four years in the Signal Corps, where he "made training movies. Did hitch with Charles Addams, Cobean, Saroyan." He also claimed to have painted "murals for the Fort Monmouth latrine."

He never returned to magazines after the army. In 1946 the *Archie* comic strip, daily and Sunday, began and Montana devoted all his time to that. Over the years his work became increasingly bland and hurried-looking. Montana suffered a fatal heart attack in January of 1975 while skiing near his sixteen-acre home in New Hampshire.

An exuberant and enthusiastic early *Archie* ® page. *(Copyright © 1986 Archie ® Comic Publications, Inc.)*

Klaus Nordling

Although a cartoonist for most of his life, Nordling was active in newsstand comic books for little more than a decade. He is best remembered as the artist who drew the definitive version of *Lady Luck,* which he took over in 1942 and drew off and on until 1950. He has an individual, cartoony style and a screwball sense of humor. The adventure stories he turned out in the forties were unlike anyone else's, and in their own way were as inventive and distinctive as those of his long-time colleague Will Eisner.

Nordling is a self-taught cartoonist: "I started doodling when I was a kid." He was born in Finland in 1915 and came to the United States as a child. His parents settled in Brooklyn in the area then known as Fintown. He worked for Alexander King's satiric magazine *Americana,* drew a weekly comic strip about Baron Munchausen, and got into comic books in 1939.

As Nordling recalls, he signed on with the Eisner-Iger shop at about the time it was starting up. His first assignment was *Shorty Shortcake,* a mock adventure done in animated cartoon style for Fox's *Wonderworld Comics.* He soon added more serious fare, taking over *Spark Stevens,* a strip about a daredevil sailor, from Bob Kane. This also ran in *Wonderworld.* The shop supplied the contents of the Fiction House magazine as well, and Nordling drew *Strut Warren, Powder Burns,* and *Greasemonkey Griffin* for such titles as *Fight Comics* and *Wings.* He usually worked at home, doing all the writing and drawing himself—"lettering, erasing, everything."

Fairly prolific in the early 1940s, he contributed *Crash, Cork & the Baron*—"three flyers in the old 'bunch of pals' adventure tradition"—to *Speed Comics* and an unlikely superhero named the Thin Man to Marvel's *Mystic Comics.* Through Eisner he also began working for the Quality line. He did *Bob & Swab* in *Hit Comics, Shot & Shell* in *Military,* and *Kid Dixon* in *National.* His most successful creation was *Pen Miller,* which ran in *National* and then *Cracks.* Pen was a cartoonist-detective, a "nemesis of the underworld." Nordling admits the blond pipe-smoking sleuth was loosely based on himself. "I never had adventures like that. But, yes, everybody said he looked like me."

Lady Luck, alias socialite Brenda Banks, had made her debut in the weekly *Spirit* section in 1940. When Nick Cardy, the second artist on the feature, was drafted in 1942, Eisner summoned Nordling to take over. Eisner's studio was in Manhattan. "They were in a jam," Nordling recalls. "So I dashed off in the middle of winter, left my wife and kids in Minnesota, to come take over *Lady Luck."* He hadn't been following the adventures of the debutante Robin Hood, and Eisner didn't give him much in the way of advice. "He just showed me a couple of strips from before. . . . I just studied them and mulled it over for awhile. And thought, well, this stuff is too straight. I liked to have a little comedy in there . . . so I suggested what I'd like to do with it to Will. And he said, 'Sure, go ahead.' " What Nordling did was convert the feature to a screwball mystery-comedy, mixing crime and satire. Historian Catherine Yronwode has said that he's the one "whom most fans think of as the definitive Lady Luck artist."

He stayed with the character initially for four years, turning out over 200 four-page adventures before stepping aside. Like Eisner, Nordling became fascinated with integrating his logo into the splash panel, and one of the pleasures of following the weekly episodes was in seeing how the words "Lady Luck" would fit into both the design of the page and the opening of the story. Commencing with #42 (April, 1943), *Lady Luck* was reprinted in *Smash Comics.* She outlasted the magazine, which became *Lady Luck* with #86 (December, 1949). Nordling returned to the strip at this point, contributing new stories to the magazine's five issues.

The Barker was a somewhat unlikely comic book hero. Created by Jack Cole and writer Joseph Millard, he first showed up in *National* #42 (May, 1944). Nordling took over the drawing and writing shortly thereafter. This strip about a traveling circus, its personnel, and its unusual adventures as it moved across the country inspired Nordling to some of his most ambitious, and amusing, stories. *National* folded a few months before *Lady Luck,* and by 1950 Nordling was out of comic books.

Or at least traditional comics. He spent the next several years working with Eisner on industrial and educational comic books. Still active today, he devotes most of his time to commercial cartooning.

LADY LUCK

By Klaus Nordling

JUSTIN WAS DEAD WHEN WE GOT HERE... SAME OLD STORY... SMOKING A CIGARETTE IN BED... THE BED CAUGHT ON FIRE....

OH, JOY! TO AN AMUSEMENT PARK I HAVE NEVER BEEN!

I'M A LITTLE CURIOUS ABOUT THE NATURE OF THAT FIRE...

HERE EES PACKAGE OF VEECTEEM'S SMOKES... ROYAL FLUSH CEEGARETS...

HM...

THIS BURNED STUB UNDER THE BED IS ANOTHER BRAND... MEDAL!

NOW WHATEVER HAPPENED TO THAT COUNT AGAIN?

HEES WANDER OFF TO THE SIDE-SHOW, I'MA SUPPOSE...

FASCINATING!

PHOTO? ONLY A QUARTER!

I DO NOT HAVE A QUARTER...

LILA THE BEARDED LADY

Imaginative layouts plus the characteristic Nordling sense of humor. *(Copyright © 1986 Will Eisner.)*

George Pérez

He's come a long way in the past ten years. Pérez's entry in *The Who's Who of American Comic Books,* published in 1975, took up only six lines. In the years since then he's added considerably to his list of credits and to his reputation. During the Golden Age of the 1940s, artists and writers labored unheralded and unsung. Today, with an abundance of fanzines and specialty publications around, that situation has changed. Pérez is one of the fan's favorite artists, and only John Byrne has been able to beat him in the polls. *Comics Scene* once said, "He has helped redefine the way team comics are handled and has brought back some of the energy and excitement missing from the comics." *Amazing Heroes* described his work as having both "power and subtlety."

He is a product of the comics generation, self-taught and inspired originally by the art he saw in the comic books themselves. "I've been drawing since I was five years old," he's said. An early favorite of his was Superman as rendered by the dependable Curt Swan. A later influence, one he was exposed to in his teens, was Jack Kirby's Marvel work. "Starting from Swan, I went through a Kirby period and even Steve Ditko—very briefly, I just loved the way Ditko did hands," he says. "Then others that followed were Steranko, Neal Adams, Barry Smith, Gil Kane, Mort Drucker, and many others."

Pérez was born in the South Bronx and in the early 1970s began to attend comics conventions in the Manhattan area. He was able to show his samples to professionals, and in 1973 he was hired to assist Rich Buckler. After parting with Buckler, Pérez starting pencilling directly for Marvel. "When Marvel got a hole in their schedule," he's explained, "they suddenly had no one to draw a feature that no one wanted to draw anyway. They gave it to me." The feature was *Man-Wolf* in *Creatures on the Loose* and, fairly soon, the magazine's sales picked up. Shortly thereafter Pérez graduated to such better-known heroes as the Fantastic Four and the Avengers. "Looking back," he says of his work from that period, "my style was pretty much Marvel house style— very large, thick characters, very musclebound, not very flexible. But I was learning to do layouts and all of a sudden I developed a reputation. The subtleties I developed later were absent, but the power was definitely there." He also feels that another thing he had going for him was "a natural storytelling ability which seemed to transcend most of the flaws in my drawing."

Pérez continued to be an impressive and productive penciller for the next several years, but then he reached a point where he had to stop for a while. "It felt great doing all those books, but I think it might have been too much for any one person to take on." Part of his comeback effort was the work he did on both the *X-Men* and *Fantastic Four* annuals in the late 1970s. He then teamed up with editor-writer Marv Wolfman to rejuvenate the venerable Teen Titans. Pérez changed with his job and he feels he was able "to prove I can handle stories with characters and characterization, as opposed to always having slam-bang action." The *New Teen Titans* became a runaway hit. And, as *Amazing Heroes* puts it, "The *Titans* have gone on to achieve a place in the hearts of fans, enthusiasts, and pros alike that had not been achieved by a new DC book for many, many years . . . a far-reaching series whose simplicity and involvement have attracted new fans and rejuvenated the interest of old readers."

Pérez gave up the Titans in 1984 to work with Wolfman on *Crisis on Infinite Earths,* the maxiseries designed to redefine the DC universe. More ambitious in scope and casting than both parts of Marvel's *Secret Wars* combined, the book has given Pérez ample opportunity to be both powerful and subtle. The issues are full of action, characterization ("The characters move in the way characters should move, in contrast to everyone having interchangeable poses," says Pérez), vast and detailed landscapes, and seascapes and cityscapes. Pérez is also a master of crowd control. In this maxiseries in particular he has been able to jam dozens of DC heroes and heroines into some of his panels and still make each and every one of them a recognizable individual. After *Crisis,* he plans to do more special projects, graphic novels, and a new version of *Wonder Woman.*

It looks like his comeback will be permanent.

A rare Pérez page from Man-Wolf, his first professional solo feature. Script by David Kraft, inks by R. Villamonte. *(Copyright © 1978 Marvel Comics Group.)*

Wendy Pini

The earliest attention Pini gained from comic book fans was for a rather unusual achievement. Her celebrity resulted not from her writing, her pencilling, or her inking, but from dressing up like Red Sonja and appearing in some of the shows Frank Thorne was staging at East Coast comics conventions in the late 1970s. Thorne himself portrayed the Wizard, decked out in a Merlin outfit, and Pini donned a metal-and-wire bikini that weighed approximately nine pounds. Some of the earliest mentions of her most important achievement in the field appeared in fanzine and newspaper accounts of those sword-and-sorcery shows. One such, for instance, said of her, "She is also a comic artist whose latest work is the 'Elfquest' character to be published next year."

Elfquest, which deals not with a single character but with an entire imagined world, first appeared in 1978 as a black-and-white alternate press comic book. Its subsequent sales have been most impressive and Pini, aided by her husband Richard, has achieved the sort of success with her homemade comic book that seems typically American—the sort of thing brought off in earlier generations by pioneering dreamers who invented a new kind of automobile or sewing machine.

"I came up with the idea for *Elfquest* in 1977," she explained in 1984, "presented the idea to Richard, and he liked it. I began drawing the series without any real idea of how we were going to get it published. We took a package to both Marvel and DC. They rejected it as not being commercial enough." The first issue was finally brought out by an alternate publisher, but the Pinis were not happy with the deal. "We decided we would gamble and publish ourselves. Fortunately, we knew two distributors who were both very supportive. . . . With a little financial help from friends and relatives, we borrowed money to get off the ground. We put out our first issue with a press run of 10,000. Both distributors bought the entire run, and *Elfquest* took off. Since then, every issue has increased its press run, and we were able to pay back our loan within two months. 10,000 is high for a beginning project like that, but now we're over 50,000."

Pini's fantasy world and her appealing characters—Leetah, Cutter, etc.—proved to be marketable. Posters, a novel, albums, and reprints followed the comic book. The critical reaction to her work was also favorable for the most part. Writing in *The Comics Journal* in the spring of 1982, Jan Strnad said, "Wendy depends more on minor detail than on major revelations to give her characters life, showing us the way they move, stand, sit, fidget, and engage in their day-to-day activities. . . . Like a well-crafted film that draws us into the story and manipulates our emotions without obvious artifice, Wendy's *Elfquest* solicits our sympathies quietly, unobtrusively." By 1984 *Amazing Heroes* was enthusiastic enough to proclaim that Elfquest was "one of the most radically original and widely acclaimed works of fiction of the past twenty years." They added, "It's far more than the tale of how elves first came among humans . . . what *Elfquest* presents us with is a world peopled by our most intrinsic selves, unchained from the uniform pettiness of this world and living the utmost heights of dream."

She's been singled out as "the first woman successfully to present her own epic-length series in the comic book field." Pini is aware that she's thrived in an area that was long considered to be for men (and boys) only. "The nature of the comic book audience has changed over the past twenty years," she says. *"Elfquest* boasts the highest percentage of female readers of any comics series currently on the market. I say this with ill-concealed pride and the results of a widesweeping demographic survey in hand. *Elfquest*'s audience is, in fact, almost equally divided between male and female readers in their late teens and early twenties. Whether this trend will continue with *Elfquest*'s newsstand distribution as a Marvel/Epic reprint remains to be seen, but I suspect the pattern will hold."

A quiet moment with the elves says more than words could. *(Copyright © 1986 Warp Graphics, Inc.)*

Bob Powell

Late in the 1930s Stanley Pulowski of Buffalo, New York, came to Manhattan. He changed his name to Bob Powell and began a career in comics that lasted nearly three decades. Almost from the start Powell had a distinctive and completely professional style. That and the fact that he was fast and enterprising contributed to his becoming one of the most widely published artists in the business. He eventually drew for just about every kind of comic book—jungle girl, Western, superhero, romance, horror, etc.—and a list of his credits once compiled by a dedicated fan fills eight pages.

Powell's earliest credits are for work he did while at the Eisner-Iger shop. He drew such features as *Dr. Fung* in *Wonderworld Comics, D-13, Secret Agent* in *Mystery Men,* and *Landor, Maker of Monsters* in *Speed Comics.* He did *Gale Allen* for *Planet Comics* and *Sheena,* his best-known early character, for *Jumbo.* It was on these latter strips that Powell began to demonstrate his affinity for drawing pretty women, a knack he would refine and develop over the years.

When Eisner split with his partner to start a small shop of his own, he said, "I took some of the good artists." Among them were Lou Fine and Powell. During this association Powell drew a variety of features, mostly for the Quality line—two of his specialties were women and airplanes—and contributed a weekly four-page adventure of *Mr. Mystic* to Eisner's just-launched *Spirit* booklet. This one he also wrote. He parted with Eisner in the early 1940s, apparently because he was unhappy over his page rates, and went out on his own. In 1942 he began an association with the Harvey Brothers that was to last for fifteen years. He was particularly effective with pretty girl characters like Black Cat and the Blonde Bomber. Powell's women were getting sexier and more zaftig. They were usually wide-shouldered, long-haired, long-legged, and full-chested, borrowing attributes from such 1940s movie goddesses as Rita Hayworth, Betty Grable, and Jane Russell.

Powell entered the service in 1943. "I was hot to be a flyer, so before I got too goddam ancient, I enlisted," he once recalled. He eventually became an air force instructor, "which kept me out of the shooting war." He was able to do some cartooning while in the service and returned to it just as soon as he was mustered out in 1945. "I was still in uniform when the Harveys put me right back to work." Perhaps inspired by memories of his days with Eisner, he now set up a shop of his own, based in his Long Island home. "I had had an assistant before the war and now, with things booming, I took on several more. . . . I did the writing, pencilling, and the faces. Howard Nostrand and Marty Epp did the inking. Marty also did lettering. George Siefringer did backgrounds. Other casuals did cleanup, errands, and created ulcers."

The shop did considerable work for such Harvey titles as *Speed Comics* and nearly dominated the Street & Smith titles of the late 1940s. Powell and associates drew the Shadow—providing the sexiest Margo Lane ever seen in any medium—Doc Savage, Red Dragon, and a Nick Carter that has been called the definitive one. Powell got up samples for a Nick Carter newspaper strip at this same time, but it never sold. The Powell product of these years was more imaginatively laid out and much more lushly inked, perhaps due in part to the inking of the late Howard Nostrand.

One of Powell's most interesting creations of this period was *The Man in Black.* Essentially comic book versions of the strange and sardonic tales to be heard on radio shows like *The Whistler* and *Suspense,* the stories were narrated by a shadowy tuxedoed and caped figure also known as Fate. They appeared as fillers in assorted Harvey magazines, and the continuities were nicely staged, rich with unsettling angles and ominous shadows.

Powell continued in the fifties and sixties to turn out an enormous amount of work, including a short-lived revival of *The Man in Black* in the mid 1950s. He was also responsible for *Bobby Benson's B-Bar-B Riders, Jet Powers, Cave Girl, Thund'da, Sub-Mariner, The Hulk, Robin Hood, Red Hawk,* an adaptation of *The Red Badge of Courage,* and even a comic book about Pope Pius XII.

In addition he put in a year on the *Bat Masterson* comic strip ("I hated it"), drew gum cards for Topps, and served as art director for *Sick.* During his last years he worked in commercial art, bitter that the collapse of a great many of his comic book publishers had left him in a rough position. "Finally I was able to break the style of drawing and started earning a decent living and again a damn good one . . . but, oh, do I remember the years of struggle when art directors would say, 'Ah, yes. Very nice, Mr. Powell, but you were a *comic book* artist, weren't you?' "

He died in 1967.

Some of his specialties on display—pretty girls, jungle scenery, and mystical heroes. *(Copyright © 1986 Will Eisner.)*

Mac Raboy

One of the most impressive artists, and undisputably the slowest, of the Golden Age was Emanual "Mac" Raboy. Born in New York City in 1916, he got his art training in Work Projects Administration classes during the Depression years. He did his first professional work for WPA projects, then got a job with a small commercial art service, where he did "all kinds of the usual dirty work." In 1940 a newspaper ad lured him into the sweatshop of the enterprising Harry "A" Chesler—nicknamed "Chiseler" by some of his disgruntled employees—and he began what was to be an impressive career in comics.

Raboy's earliest stuff, back-up features in magazines such as *Prize Comics, Silver Streak, Master,* and *Whiz,* was not especially notable. It was competent and neat, showing the influence of his idol Alex Raymond, but nothing to make the average reader look twice or whistle with admiration. By 1941, though, he'd made a great leap forward. This was most noticeable on *Dr. Voodoo* in Fawcett's *Whiz Comics.* Begun by another artist, this feature had originally been about a physician who works with the natives of Africa. Soon after Raboy took over it was changed into a time-traveling fantasy and came to resemble a blend of *Flash Gordon* and *Prince Valiant.* Like these handsome Sunday pages, there were no balloons, only breathless captions—"The dragon's roars are deafening, and its breath melts the jagged stones . . . but Dr. Voodoo avoids this and lithely leaps to the ground." Raboy had found his metier. He was at his best with swashbuckling larger-than-life adventure, and his gracefully drawn and carefully inked figures were most at home in the realms of fantasy.

After working on a number of other Fawcett heroes, including Bulletman, Raboy was tapped to draw their next intended star. Captain Marvel, Jr., made his debut late in 1941 and Raboy drew most of his adventures in *Master Comics* for the next two years. He also did the covers for the magazine and for *Captain Marvel, Jr.,* which came along late the following year. Raboy's covers are some of his most impressive work. They are well designed, beautifully drawn, and often make use of rather awesome perspectives. With his boy superhero Raboy was somewhat innovative; as Steranko points out, he "scorned the well-established comic axiom which demanded all super-types be a living mass of muscle. His Captain Marvel, Jr. looked like nothing more than a fourteen-year-old."

Notoriously slow, Raboy had several other artists assisting him as he struggled to meet deadlines. Even so, more than a few jobs reached print with nearly all the Captain Marvel, Jr., figures nothing more than pasteups. A few stories started off with a bang, showing off Raboy at his bravura best, and then sagged as a lesser artist picked up the brush to rush out the rest of the yarn.

Raboy was not reknowned for the dapperness of his appearance. "He was," says Steranko, "considered a sloppy dresser by his associates, and frequently developed several days' growth of beard before shaving. A habitual chain smoker, Raboy always drew while a cigarette dangled from his mouth."

He left Fawcett in 1944 to join publisher Ken Crossen and editor H. L. Gold in their new comic book venture. Calling himself Spark Publications, prolific pulp writer and long-time editor Crossen first put out *Green Lama.* This was a character he'd created for the pulps a few years earlier and adapted to comics originally in *Prize Comics.* Raboy, who had taken a turn drawing the mystical green-clad hero in *Prize,* drew him again now along with all the magazine's covers for its unsuccessful run of eight issues. He did one especially interesting story, using doubletone paper to give depth and dimension to his artwork, but still had trouble meeting his deadlines.

Raboy was rescued from comic book deadlines in 1948, when King Features hired him to take over the *Flash Gordon* page from a weary Austin Briggs. From then on Raboy had to worry only about producing one Sunday page per week. Within a year after assuming the chore, he said, "All of a sudden, I find myself with no ambition. Oh, I'm wrapped up in the work on *Flash Gordon,* which I certainly get a kick out of, but there's no burning desire in my mind any more to do something that you could call really monumental. My monument has been built." He was alluding to the home he and his wife had built in New York's Westchester County. He stayed with *Flash Gordon* until his death in 1967. His real monument is most certainly the work he did for Fawcett in the early 1940s.

One of the many handsome covers he designed in the 1940s *(Copyright © 1944 Spark Publications, Inc.)*

Jerry Robinson

Appropriately enough for a fellow who began his comics career at the age of seventeen, Robinson's first job was working for Bob Kane on *Batman* and assisting at the birth of Robin the Boy Wonder. "I'd met Bob the summer after I graduated from high school," he's said. "In those days, white painter's jackets were very popular with college kids, and students would paint all sorts of razzmatazz on their jackets. I decorated my own, as I had been the cartoonist on my high school paper. I was wearing this jacket while waiting to play tennis at a resort when this fellow came up and asked who had drawn the cartoons. He turned out to be Bob Kane . . . and he offered me a job as his assistant if I was willing to come to New York City. It seemed a great way to pay my college expenses, so I moved to New York and transferred to Columbia. . . . I began lettering the strip and inking the backgrounds. After a while, I started to ink most of the figures as well, and pretty soon Bob would just pencil the strip and I would do the complete inking."

A natural artist, Robinson improved rapidly and was soon soloing on Batman and Robin episodes. He also began to be influenced by other cartoonists, especially the gifted Mort Meskin, with whom he shared a studio at one point. Robinson was Meskin's most successful disciple; from 1939 into the early 1940s, his artwork continually changed and improved. He eventually changed the entire look of the Batman tales, culminating in the covers and stories he did for *Batman* and *Detective Comics* in 1942 and 1943. He'd developed a personalized way of drawing figures, one that mixed the heroic with a slight fantasy element, and his staging was both inventive and effective. Most of all, Robinson gave the impression he was enjoying himself.

Robinson drew a war-oriented mystery man known as London for the original *Daredevil* in 1941. This was the first thing he got to sign his name to. London worked in Europe and specialized in thwarting Nazi spies, saboteurs, and supervillains. By the middle 1940s Robinson had left *Batman* and was drawing the *Green Hornet* for the Harvey Brothers. In 1946 he drew an up-to-date hero named Atoman—"Who is this new man whose body generates atomic power?" Atoman proved to be a dud, despite Robinson's handsome artwork, and he survived for but two issues. Robinson next teamed up with Meskin to produce some striking stories for such heroes as the Vigilante, the Black Terror, the Fighting Yank, and Johnny Quick. These jobs were usually pencilled by Meskin and inked by Robinson. The 1950s found him doing war, crime, and horror for Marvel as well as *Lassie* and *Bat Masterson* for Western. By the time he left comics in the early 1960s his style had become calmer and a bit sedate.

In the fall of 1953 Robinson had done his first newspaper strip, for the New York *Herald Tribune*'s syndicate. *Jet Scott* offered science fiction in a contemporary setting with a lanky, dark-haired hero who was "not a ray-blasting space ranger but a scientific investigator for the Pentagon." The scripts were by Sheldon Stark, a veteran of both comics and radio. Robinson brought the style he had been developing in comic books to the project, refining it some. *Jet Scott* had a sophisticated look, and the women who inhabited it were slim and stylish. Like many a Pentagon employee, Jet didn't limit himself to home-ground adventures. He also journeyed to exotic locales such as Saudi Arabia and the South Seas, all of which Robinson depicted in his best cinematic fashion. Despite its good looks, the strip folded in just under two years.

Robinson began to turn his back on adventure in the sixties. He did a humor panel, *Still Life,* in which inanimate objects held conversations (Check Book: The bank was robbed . . . how much did they get? Pen: 57 toasters, 42 electric blankets, 69 pressure cookers, and 145 bath mats!). For the New York *News,* he commenced a funny Sunday page, still running, called *Flubbs & Fluffs,* illustrating bloopers allegedly made in the classroom and elsewhere. In the 1970s he self-syndicated *Life With Robinson,* a satirical strip commenting on current life and politics. Robinson is a past president of the National Cartoonist Society and the author of a history of comic strips. All in all, he is a man of many accomplishments. For many, however, his greatest accomplishment was his comic book work of the 1940s.

One of the relatively few superguys created in the middle 1940s. *(Copyright © 1946 Spark Publications.)*

John Romita, Sr.

Romita is another artist whose career was permanently affected by his association with Spider-Man. According to *Comics Scene,* he is "the artist most identified with Spider-Man, with the possible exception of Steve Ditko. . . . Romita's style set the tone for every Spider-Man artist to follow." *The World Encyclopedia of Comics* is even more enthusiastic, saying, "Romita brought *Spider-Man* in line with the rest of Marvel's handsomely illustrated titles. . . . Whereas Ditko's *Spider-Man* was populated by everyday people, Romita's *Spider-Man* was populated by noble-bearing and majestic-looking characters." Interestingly enough Romita had been drawing everyday people himself, in such DC titles as *Girls' Love Stories, Secret Hearts,* and *Falling In Love,* before taking over Spidey.

He was born in Brooklyn in 1930 and started drawing soon after. "I used to . . . copy my favorite comic strips like *Dick Tracy* and *Terry and the Pirates.* Later I went on to do Disney characters. Before I was ten years old, I was doing drawings of all the *Tracy, Terry,* and Disney characters. . . . At that age, I didn't know if I wanted to be a cartoonist or not. I remember sending a batch of my samples to the New York *News* when I was about eleven. They sent me a warm letter of encouragement. They told me that Chester Gould had a contract with them to do *Tracy* and therefore they couldn't really take him off the strip to put me on it."

After attending Manhattan's High School of Industrial Arts, he broke into comics in 1949 by doing romance stories for magazines published by the Famous Funnies folks. His long association with Marvel began the following year. In those early years Romita worked in just about every category going in that period before the superheroes came back—crime, romance, horror, jungle, science fiction, etc. He's said, "In this business you must be able to handle anything that comes your way. The superheroes may be very big today. But it's quite possible in a few years that there won't be any superhero comic books. Instead it might be Westerns or a combination of soap opera and science fiction." Throughout the 1950s and into the 1960s he certainly demonstrated his versatility. Besides the above genres, Romita also tried

his hand at such cowboy titles as *Kid Colt* and *Western Kid.* And when Captain America made a brief comeback in 1954, both in his own magazine and in *Young Men,* Romita was the artist. This was his first chance to depict a superhero.

During a slump in Marvel business in the late fifties Romita went to work for DC, producing mostly romance material. By 1965 he was back at his alma mater again and was swept up in the new wave of popularity for superheroes. After inking *The Avengers,* pencilling *Daredevil,* and working on *Captain America* once again, Romita took over the *Amazing Spider-Man* book with #39 (September, 1966). He remained with the character, off and on, for the next seven years. He was, like Kirby and Buscema, an influential artist, and he had a great deal to do with the overall look of Marvel comics in the seventies. In 1972 he was appointed art director for Marvel. While this decreased his output, it increased his influence.

The ever-growing popularity of the character prompted the Register and Tribune Syndicate to introduce an *Amazing Spider-Man* strip in the middle 1970s. Romita was the initial artist on the feature, which at its peak was appearing in several hundred newspapers across the country. Interviewed in *Cartoonist PROfiles* in 1978, he was not wildly enthusiastic about the venture. "It's still a problem to me to accept the format change," he complained, "from a twenty-pager to daily strips and Sunday pages. The comic books give you a chance to use a lot of tricky storytelling and graphic gimmicks. . . . You don't have to begin and end a characterization in one story. . . . I miss the luxury of panoramic action shots and the full-page spreads." Not surprisingly, Romita quit the strip before much more time had passed.

Now the art director at Marvel, he has returned to Spidey on a few occasions, inking comic book pages pencilled by his son John, Jr. "I wish I had the time to do more with him," he's said. "If I were willing to give up my nine-to-five job, I think I could do steady work with him. But I'm trying to avoid getting back into the rat race, turning out a lot of pages every week. I just don't have the energy for that anymore."

Romita's dramatic portrayal of Spider-Man. Script by Stan Lee, inks by Mike Esposito.
(Copyright © 1966 Marvel Comics Group.)

Alex Schomburg

Schomburg's work exemplified the maxim that you can't judge a book by its cover, since his comic book covers were often livelier and better drawn than anything to be found inside the magazines they graced. He was inventive, untiring, and sometimes subtly whimsical. The master of controlled clutter, he was the Hieronymous Bosch of comics and filled his drawings with dozens of figures, weapons, infernal machines, and enough action for at least a year of ordinary covers.

His most memorable efforts were for Marvel in the years just before and during the Second World War. In his late thirties when he began producing covers, Schomburg became an expert at depicting Captain America, the Human Torch, and Sub-Mariner, singly or as a team, in the most complex and improbable situations. His spectacular and intricate covers appeared on *Marvel Mystery Comics, Human Torch, Sub-Mariner, All Winners,* and *Young Allies.*

There was usually no single center of attention on one of his bright covers; they were more like three-ring circuses, with Sub-Mariner pulling down a bridge and causing Nazi troops and tanks to go plummeting into a ravine in one corner, the Human Torch saving Bucky from being fed into a blast furnace in another, and Cap parachuting down and blasting away at a dozen or so hooded Japanese spies with a tripod machine gun. You could browse through a Schomburg cover, savoring the weapons and fiendish devices, the multiplicity of perils about to befall Toro, Bucky, or some hapless damsel, the hordes of faithfully rendered Axis troops, the explosions and fireworks. The artist, with his bravura style, always convinced you that all the action and noise he crammed into a cover could actually be occurring at that single frozen instant of time. He was an expert at a sort of wild

and woolly pageantry, and his covers made perfect packaging for the Marvel wartime titles.

Schomburg also turned out covers for *Exciting Comics, Thrilling, Black Terror,* and such Harvey titles as *Speed Comics, All New,* and *Green Hornet.* The covers of most of the Harvey comics came with a two-page printed explanation inside—called *The Story Behind The Cover*—and the writer who could fit the whole story of a Schomburg cover into that limited space was indeed a master of compression. During his decade and more in the field he did very little interior work, the most notable job being *Jon Juan.* This was a 1950 feature starring a super lover, with script by Jerry Siegel, and it lasted exactly one issue.

Schomburg never worked directly inside a publishing house. "I had my own small studio over on Eighth Avenue and Forty-fourth Street," he once explained. "In that manner I was able to do work for the competition such as Ned Pines's Standard Magazines, for whom I signed the art 'Xela.'" He usually had a free hand. "I seldom submitted pencil roughs. They bought sight unseen, just as long as the Japs showed their ugly teeth and glasses and the Nazis looked like bums." An average cover took a week to do and the usual pay was $40 each.

After leaving comics in the early 1950s, Schomburg devoted his time to working as an illustrator for hardcover books and for science fiction magazines like *Amazing Stories* and *Isaac Asimov's.* In recent years he's returned to the complexity and clutter of yesteryear by doing some very handsome paintings based on his Golden Age covers. In them Captain America, the Human Torch, and Sub-Mariner once again face unprecedented, and lovingly rendered, perils and perplexities.

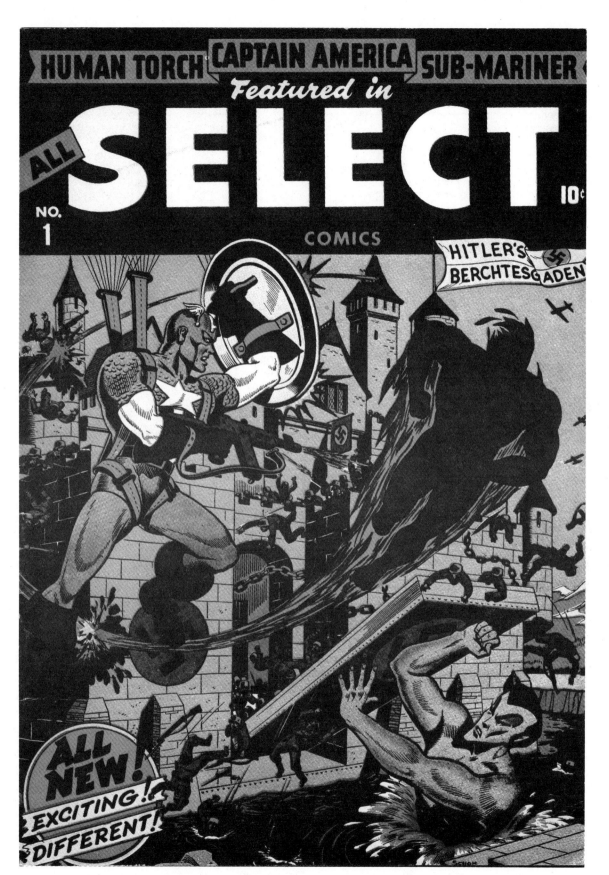

Yet another impressively cluttered wartime cover. *(Copyright © 1943 Daring Comics, Inc. and Marvel Comics Group.)*

John Severin

Throughout his career, which started in 1947, Severin has had very little to do with superheroes. A dedicated realist, he's at his best when dealing with more down-to-earth adventure. The Old West and the battlefields of various wars have been the favorite subjects for his macho drawing style. Appropriately enough some of his most characteristic work appeared in *Two-Fisted Tales*.

He was born in New Jersey in 1921 and studied at Manhattan's High School of Music and Art. He lists Roy Crane's *Captain Easy* as one of his major influences. "He could do anything," Severin's said of Crane. "Roy Crane did adventure with a beautiful combination of cartooning and storytelling." Severin's first professional work was done for the Prize group, chiefly for *Prize Comics Western*. For that title he drew, usually with Bill Elder inking, the Black Bull ("The Black Bull's war cry was 'Moo!' "), the Lazo Kid, and American Eagle, who became the cover-featured star of the magazine. On the Indian strip particularly, Severin worked hard to get the look and feel of the period. He also got involved in the writing. "The later American Eagle," he's explained, "when it started to get a little authenticity in the story line, when you got a feeling of realism in the story and when it wasn't just tomahawks and cavalry sabers, it was about then that I began taking a hand."

In 1951 he and Elder added EC to their list of markets. They did fantasy and science fiction—including some adaptions of Ray Bradbury stories—for *Weird Fantasy* and war tales for *Frontline Combat*. Severin has suggested that he and Elder teamed up originally "because we both supplied what the other guy needed. He couldn't draw and I couldn't ink." Severin was less than serious about this appraisal of their respective talents and eventually both of them went out on their own. It was for *Two-Fisted Tales* that Severin began inking his own pages. His inking style, harsher than Elder's, was choppy, giving the impression he was engraving his drawings on the page. This provided a bolder look that fit in with the tone of the magazine, with the grim Foreign Legion yarns and the low-key and gritty Western stories. Severin was allowed to edit several issues of *Two-Fisted,* and he drew every single story in #s 37, 38, and 39.

After the demise of EC in the middle fifties, Severin worked for several other publishers, including Marvel and DC. His specialties remained cowboys and soldiers: Sgt. Rock, Kid Colt, the Ringo Kid, Combat Casey, Billy the Kid, and Sgt. Fury. On this last character Severin started off pencilling and inking, but as he explains, "Stan Lee and I got together and he said, 'How would you like to take this book?' It was *Sgt. Fury* and I said, 'Swell.' And after three or issues he said, I forget what, it was some reason like, 'Gee, Severin, you're rotten.' So then Dick Ayres pencilled and I inked."

In 1958 he began a long and continuing association with *Cracked,* one of the more successful black-and-white *Mad* imitators. Severin, who'd also worked for *Mad* itself, did interior stuff and a great many full-color covers, drawing in a lighter version of his basic style. From the 1960s on he provided ambitious black-and-white stories for the Warren titles—*Eerie, Creepy,* and the short-lived *Blazing Combat.* He once said his favorite material was that drawn for EC, *Cracked,* and Warren. "And the main reason for that is simply that you have the most free expression with them."

Severin teamed with his sister Marie in the early 1970s to draw Marvel's Conan spin-off *Kull the Conqueror.* This barbarian, even with eight of his fifteen issues produced by the Severins, didn't thrive. When adventure of a wild and woolly sort has tried for a comeback, Severin has usually been there. He contributed to the unsuccessful Atlas black-and-white *Thrilling Adventure Stories* in 1975. And he showed up when Marvel launched its full-color *Amazing High Adventure* in 1985. Editor Carl Potts spoke of him reverentially in his introductory remarks, saying, "For decades John Severin has been one of the best and most respected comics artists in the business. . . . I'm happy to present his work here, with a job John has jam-packed with authentic detail." More recently he has done work for Marvel's newly revived *Savage Tales.*

In an interview some years ago Severin said, "Not too long ago somebody asked me for an interview and I said, 'Send me some questions.' And one of his questions was, who did I think had the most outstanding technique in the comics field. And I said, 'Me.' Because I don't think that anybody else in the field is crazy enough to do it that way."

Western action and human drama, Severin style. Script by Charles Dixon. *(Copyright © 1985 Marvel Comics Group.)*

Joe Shuster

Superman—along with Tarzan, Sherlock Holmes, Dracula, etc.—is a character compelling enough to thrive without any help from his original creators. And like Clark Kent, Joe Shuster has always been overshadowed by Superman. Shuster is well-known and much written about simply because he is the cocreator of the most successful comic book character of all time. Yet his actual work, his drawing style, is usually either ignored or dismissed. Appraising Shuster's art has proven difficult for those who have tried, because once Superman became popular a shop was set up to meet the accelerating demand for material. Shuster signed his name to everything coming out of the shop, including work done by Paul Cassidy, Leo Novack, John Sikela, and Wayne Boring.

To understand and appreciate Shuster's accomplishments as a cartoonist and the innovations he brought to the fledgling comic book business, you have to go back to the middle 1930s, to the years before the Man of Steel had leaped over a single skyscraper or raced against his first locomotive, when Shuster and his long-time friend Jerry Siegel were breaking into comics.

Siegel and Shuster began selling to comic books when there were only a few titles being published. In fact, they sold two features to *More Fun Comics*—initially called *New Fun*—in 1935, the pioneering magazine's first year in business. This book, put together by the enterprising and usually impecunious Major Malcolm Wheeler-Nicholson, was the first, with a couple of unsuccessful earlier exceptions, to use original material. Up until the Major came along comic books had been content to reprint newspaper strips. The earliest work of the Cleveland-based artist-and-writer team seems to be unsold Sunday page ideas. The features were *Henri Duval,* about a swashbuckling French swordsman, and *Dr. Occult,* starring a ghost detective.

Although they couldn't sell Superman, a character they'd cooked up while still in high school, the team did place several other features with Major Nicholson: *Federal Men* in *New Comics, Radio Squad* in *More Fun,* and *Spy* and *Slam Bradley* in *Detective.* Siegel has said, *"Slam Bradley* was a dry run for *Superman . . .* we just couldn't resist putting into *Slam Bradley* some of the slam-bang stuff which we knew would be in *Superman."* Shuster adds, "We turned it out with no restrictions, complete freedom to do what we wanted. The only problem was we had a deadline. We had to work very fast, so Jerry suggested that we save time by putting less than six panels to a page: four panels or three panels, and sometimes two panels. I think one day we just had one panel to a page. The kids loved it because it was spectacular. I could do so much more. Later on, the editors stopped us from doing that. They said the kids were not getting their money's worth."

What Shuster is talking about here, in his self-effacing way, is how he changed the format of comic books. Almost all his contemporaries in those early days were striving to look like newspaper strips and Sunday pages. Shuster was among the first to realize that a comic book page is not a newspaper page. He broke his up in new and interesting ways and was one of the first comic book artists to use a full-page splash panel to lead off his stories. These panels were often more like posters, touting the story to come rather than offering the opening scene. The newspaper artist who seems to have had the most influence on Shuster was Roy Crane, who was also breaking away from traditional layouts in his *Captain Easy* Sunday pages. Shuster's appealing, concise style, with its cartoony overtones, is a personal variation on Crane's.

Another important influence on Shuster was the movies. He's said he was inspired by them "as far as the composition of different scenes. You know, the long shot, the close-up. In my mind's eye I was creating a movie and playing all the parts. I would become an actor . . . and the director as well."

For the most part Shuster was self-taught. "I had very little formal training. I think it was natural talent. I began drawing when I was about four years old, I've been told. I did take some school courses in drawing, illustration and anatomy." As he recalls the early comic book features weren't drawn under ideal conditions. "I had no drawing board at the time, no art supplies. My mother gave me her bread board to work on when she wasn't using it. . . . When I had no paper, sometimes I would use brown wrapping paper. I remember once I found several rolls of wallpaper. I was overjoyed. The back was white and I had enough drawing paper to supply me for a long time." Recalling *Henri Duval* and *Dr. Occult,* Shuster says, "One was done on brown paper and one on wallpaper. When it was sold, they told us to redraw it and we went out and bought good paper."

In 1938 he and Siegel succeeded in selling *Superman* to *Action Comics* and that changed Shuster's life for good and all.

But that's another story.

Dr. Mystic appeared exactly once, in *Funny Pages*. (Copyright © 1936 Comics Magazine Company, Inc.)

Bill Sienkiewicz

Sienkiewicz has learned on the job. In a half-dozen years in comic books he's moved from being a sedulous imitator of others to being an artist with a highly individual style all his own. He's also become a very forceful painter and his covers provide attractive packaging for many Marvel titles and for DC's line of science fiction graphic novels. In a recent *Comics Buyer's Guide* poll he placed third on the list of favorite artists, and the book he'd been devoting most of his time to, *The New Mutants,* was among the top ten on the favorite comic list.

Only a few years ago Sienkiewicz was not as highly thought of. Back in 1982, for example, *The Comics Journal* dismissed him as someone whose "art leans heavily on lessons learned from Neal Adams." They concluded that "Sienkiewicz seems to have learned to draw by studying Adams, period." Sienkiewicz acknowledges the Adams influence, saying in a recent interview, "While Neal's stuff used to have such an incredible effect on me, it really doesn't anymore."

He's been a comics fan since early childhood. "I guess I was about six years old," he recalls. "I started reading comics just about the time I started to draw—I may even have started drawing them before I started reading them. . . . I pretty much started just from being bored, basically. I guess that's how *every* kid starts." His favorite artists in his youth were Jack Kirby and Curt Swan. "And oddly enough, when Neal first came on the scene, I couldn't stomach his stuff. . . . It wasn't until later, when he started doing interior stuff, that I started to catch on. It was an acquired taste." Sienkiewicz drew comic book pages while in high school, strictly for his own amusement and that of his friends. In college he studied illustration and advertising.

His first regular assignment in comics came in 1980, when he was signed by Marvel to draw *Moon Knight.* He says he got the job by simply walking in and showing his portfolio, which contained mostly drawings of DC characters. "It started out looking a lot like Neal's stuff," he says, "and it took almost fifteen to twenty issues before I felt it really had a look of its own." He credits the frequent comparisons to Adams, some less than flattering, with pushing him on to work out a style, a way of telling stories, that was his alone. "It bugged me," he says. "It started to brew and finally came to some kind of a head around *Moon Knight #23,* when there were all these feelings of frustration and a desire to cut loose and start relying on things that were patently me." It was while drawing *Moon Knight* that he started experimenting with covers: trying unconventional layouts, working entirely in black and white. With the thirtieth issue he left the book.

There followed a period where he did mostly covers. "I'd gotten the painting bug," he explains. "I felt like my black-and-white work was getting up to a certain level and my painting was way down here." Eventually Sienkiewicz settled in for a run with *The New Mutants.* He did the interior work—both pencilling and inking—and painted the covers. His layouts became increasingly audacious and he threw in every sort of technique from Craftint to spatter. The artwork showed the influence of a wide range of artists, including Bob Peak, Ralph Steadman, and Gustav Klimt. He's admitted that initially he wasn't enthusiastic about the assignment, but then he got to thinking "maybe these bland-looking characters in this incredibly chiaroscuro kind of world, if nothing else, would be a chance to play with design and pattern and motifs. . . . I just started to add lighting, shadows, and stuff. All of a sudden I found myself being interested in certain characters and it just became fun to do."

In addition to comics, Sienkiewicz has drawn for the *National Lampoon* and magazines like *Golf Digest.* In 1985 he gave up *The New Mutants* to devote himself to special projects and graphic novels for Marvel. Asked to explain how he approached his work, he replied, "I'm trying to say, look, this is life, this is fun . . . I think that's pretty much what my work is an expression of . . . it's so much fun."

The New Mutants enter Sienkewicz's bizarre dreamworld. Script by Chris Claremont.
(Copyright © 1985 Marvel Comics Group.)

Walt Simonson

It wasn't until Simonson had been in comics for ten years that he produced a "hot title." That occurred in 1983, when he became artist and writer on Marvel's *Thor*. He'd been associated with successful characters before—Batman, Fantastic Four, etc.—but his contributions hadn't boosted their sales appreciably. When *Thor* #337 (November, 1983) hit the stands, however, things were different and the magazine sold out in shops across the country. Even Simonson's admirers hadn't expected that and *The Comics Journal's* headline—"Simonson Thor Success Surprises Dealers"—was typical of the reaction in the fan press. The work that brought him a larger audience was impressive, but somewhat more subdued than what he'd done earlier. Simonson himself says, "I'm doing a very conservative comic. It's a lot like it used to be, for me, and I haven't changed a lot of the characters or the visual vocabulary."

Born in Knoxville, Tennessee, Simonson had two abiding interests from childhood on—drawing and geology. When he graduated from Amherst College in Massachusetts in 1968, he decided that art was more important to him than paleontology and moved on to the Rhode Island School of Design.

His earliest professional artwork had been done for DC in the early 1970s, mostly fantasy stories for assorted titles. In the autumn of 1973 he teamed up with editor-writer Archie Goodwin to do an updated version of the venerable crimefighter Manhunter—"He stalks the world's most dangerous game!" The strip ran in *Detective Comics* from #437 through #443. Simonson's pages had a highly individual look, owing little to either the DC or the Marvel bullpen styles of the period. His people, even his improbably costumed hero, were lean and elongated. His inking was intricate and quirky, with a nervous, scratchy quality. And he experimented with page breakdowns, slicing up some into as many as thirteen panels, devoting others to just one enormous panel. He was obviously enjoying himself and thinking, perhaps just a bit too much, about how best to tell the story.

Moving to Marvel in the middle 1970s, he worked on a variety of features—*Master of Kung Fu, Battlestar Galactica, The Hulk, Star Wars,* and *Dazzler.* He even put in some time pencilling *Thor* in 1977 and 1978. He was enthusiastic about returning to the helmeted hero in 1983. "Of all the Marvel superheroes, Thor was the guy that I read first and he remained my favorite during Marvel's period of producing some great comics in the sixties," he's said. In fact, in the late 1960s his enthusiasm was such that Simonson, not yet a comics pro, wrote and drew a Thor yarn for his own amusement. "What I'm doing now is working out my fantasies from fifteen years ago. I put together a whole story at the time and I am now doing that story, in altered form."

Simonson became seriously interested in writing as well as drawing while working on *Battlestar Galactica.* "I had reached the point where I just didn't feel I was putting in as much energy as I wanted to," he recalls. "The writing provided a whole new set of problems of tying writing and drawing together in a way that is really very rarely possible when you have a different writer and an artist." As to how he got the scripting job, "We had people coming in and out of *Galactica* all the time. They finally asked me if I wanted to write it and my wife nudged me into it." His wife, Louise Simonson, was editing the magazine at the time.

When it comes to the actual drawing, what's most important to Simonson is that "the finished product has as much energy as possible." He has devised his own system of working. "I do my pages by doing small drawings on typewriter-size paper," he says. "That's where I do my thumbnail sketches. . . . I break the entire job down, panel by panel, page by page, one page of typing paper per page of art in the book—and then I put these in the Artograph and project them to blow them up to full size. . . . I will draw them as I'm tracing them. That way I'm able to keep the drawings as loose as possible as long as possible, to try to get as much energy as I can in the drawing of the finished product. Usually I script the story from the thumbnail before I actually blow it up. . . . Everything that I do is really geared to keeping the work as fluid as possible as long as I can."

An apocalyptic battle from Simonson's *Thor.* (Copyright © 1983 Marvel Comics Group.)

John Stanley

Another of the mystery men of comics, Stanley worked anonymously during his decades as an artist and writer. It was only years after the majority of his stuff was done that his identity became known, and even then it was only to dedicated fans who'd grown up with his *Little Lulu* comic books. In recent years he's gained somewhat more recognition, with the 1981 *Smithsonian Book of Comic-Book Comics* reprinting over forty pages of his work and more recently Another Rainbow announcing an ambitious reprint project.

Although Stanley is a cartoonist, it's as a writer and idea man that he's most admired. What Stanley provided, after writing and drawing the first couple of issues of *Little Lulu* (which commenced in 1945), was what amounted to rough storyboards for others to work from. Historian Mike Barrier explains the process this way. "To say that Stanley 'wrote' *Little Lulu* is actually a little deceptive, since he was responsible for more than the plots and dialogue. He sketched each story in rough form, so that he controlled the staging within each panel and the appearance and attitudes of the characters. The finished drawings were made by other cartoonists."

Stanley was born in New York in 1914. He won a scholarship to the New York School of Art. According to Don Phelps, long-time manager of comics conventions, Stanley "felt very uncomfortable there as most of his classmates were well-to-do and being a city kid, he did not really blend in." From art school he went into animation at the Manhattan-based Fleischer studios. After that he contributed to *The Mickey Mouse Magazine*.

Stanley joined editor Oscar Lebeck in the Dell-Western New York office in the early 1940s. Lebeck was also a writer-artist and it's possible that his simple, somewhat childlike drawing style influenced Stanley. Stanley's other coworkers included Dan Noonan, Dan Gromley, and Walt Kelly. "Most of the artists were mainly concerned with their own stuff and there were some petty jealousies going on here and there," Stanley has said, "but when Kelly walked into the Western office with a stack of art under his arm, everyone would stop what they were doing to read it. Everyone knew he was something speical. . . . I must admit that Walt and I painted the town many times. He was a very enjoyable guy to be with."

The Little Lulu character was created in the middle 1930s by Marge Henderson Buell and ran in a series of gag cartoons in the *Saturday Evening Post*. The red-clad little tyke branched out in the 1940s, showing up in newspaper advertising strips for Kleenex and in animated cartoons. Stanley believes he got the job of adapting the character to comic books by chance. "Oscar handed me the assignment but I'm sure it was due to no special form of brilliance that he thought I'd lend to it," he's said. "It could have been handed it to Dan Noonan, Kelly, or anyone else. I just happened to be available at the time."

Stanley remained available until the early 1960s, masterminding something like 175 issues of the magazine (whose full and official title was *Marge's Little Lulu*). He inherited Lulu's boyfriend Tubby from the original gag cartoons, but Stanley invented almost all the other characters, large and small. And, as Barrier points out, he changed Lulu from the lovable brat of the *Post* days. Eventually "Lulu herself became a 'good little girl' who outsmarted the boys, instead of triumphing through sheer brass as she had in the past. Many of the stories built around the rivalry theme are ingenious and funny, and the best of them spiral upward until the boys become the victims of a comic catastrophe."

It was these stories, drawn in variations of Stanley's simple style, that won kid readers and kept some of them fans for the rest of their lives. "What stories!" comments Phelps. "It is amazing how good the stories remained throughout the years given the limited framework that Stanley had to work with. The stories all took place within the same neighborhood confines . . . so how did they retain their freshness? A big reason is that they captured beautifully the mannerisms and slang of neighborhood kids. . . . There wasn't an issue that came out which did not contain some gesture, word inflection, or mannerism that amused and amazed the child reader because of its mirrorlike quality and which unlocked something in the adult reader's subconscious that perhaps had been resting there since childhood, needing only the Stanley nudge to work its way out."

Stanley did a good deal of other writing, and some drawing, for an assortment of Dell-Western titles, much of it about kids—*Nancy, Choo Choo Charlie, O. G. Whiz.* For a few issues of *Raggedy Ann and Andy* he wrote and drew *Peterkin Pottle,* a feature about a pint-size Walter Mitty. He left comics in the late 1960s, apparently with no regrets and some bitterness. He's evidenced no desire to return.

A wordless sample of Stanley's art. *(Copyright © 1986 Western Publishing Co.)*

James Steranko

Although his career in mainstream comic books lasted only a few years, Steranko managed to make a lasting impression. His work on the adventures of the belligerent, one-eyed Nick Fury in the late 1960s won him considerable attention and fan awards at the time. It also established a precedent for much of the innovative and experimental work done by other artists since.

Born in Pennsylvania in 1938, Steranko led a varied life before breaking into comics in 1966. He'd been a carnival pitchman, escape artist, magician, guitar player, photographer, and advertising director. "I do not consider myself an artist," he's said. "When I think about people who are really artists, I think of Reed Crandall and Neal Adams and maybe a half-dozen other people in comics who draw amazingly well. If I had to categorize myself, I would probably say that I belong in the class of storyteller."

It was the superhero boom of the middle sixties that got Steranko into comics. In 1966, while still working as an advertising art director, he sold a batch of brand new characters to Harvey. He designed the heroes and wrote the scripts, but didn't do any of the drawing. *Spyman* made it through three issues and his other creations didn't fare any better. By the end of the year he was in the Marvel fold, inking Jack Kirby's *Nick Fury, Agent of S.H.I.E.L.D.* A few issues later he took over the writing and drawing of the crusty superspy's escapades. Fans and readers were impressed, and by the spring of 1968, Nick had a magazine of his own.

An artist with wide-ranging and eclectic interests, Steranko created a personal and compelling collage to use on Nick Fury. "Everything from films, from radio, pulps, business, everything I could possibly apply from my background, including the magic I've done, the gigs I've played—everything goes into every comic story," he once explained. "Nick Fury became Steranko." Steranko used a whole bag of tricks to catch the reader's attention and, more often than not, he held it throughout the story. He mixed the Marvel style, as then personified by Kirby, with the techniques of Eisner and Krigstein, and added the flash of op art posters. His splash panels were sometimes as imaginative as those gracing *The Spirit.* He was continually experimenting with time, like Krigstein before him, cutting a tier into six or eight panels to speed up or slow down an action.

Steranko's work drew forth a great many enthusiastic responses. The late Phil Seuling said, "In a psychedelic and yet cuttingly real setting appear characters bigger than life, seething with righteous fury and romantic determination. The story excites, pulls, twists, and bites." And *The World Encyclopedia of Comics* called Nick Fury "possibly the best written and drawn strip of the decade." Not everyone, of course, was completely smitten. Looking back in the pages of *The Comics Journal* in 1979, Gary Groth opined, "Steranko's only real contribution to comics is in raising the technical level of medium to that of a James Bond movie." But even that was no mean accomplishment.

By 1969 he had ceased doing comic book pages for Marvel, supposedly because of deadline problems. In the early 1970s he drew covers for such titles as *Doc Savage* and *Fantastic Four.* He also edited *FOOM,* a short-lived magazine Marvel issued for its fans. When he abandoned Nick Fury, he started his own publishing outfit and named it Supergraphics. The company published two well-researched volumes of Steranko's yet-to-be completed history of comic books and continues to publish *Prevue*—which began life as *Comixscene* and then turned into *Mediascene.* Steranko has done a variety of art jobs over the years, including posters, book jackets, paperback covers, the graphic novel *Chandler,* and illustrations for his own magazine. When asked some years ago to give advice to young artists, he replied by quoting what a commercial artist had once told him. "He said, 'Make sure that your work is so goddamn good that when you go to a company, they can't afford not to hire you. They can't afford to let the competition get you!' "

Steranko's innovative layouts made comics history. Inks by Frank Giacoia. *(Copyright © 1967 Marvel Comics Group.)*

Frank Thorne

He began his professional life as a disciple of Alex Raymond, whom he imitated pretty well. This led to Thorne's drawing the *Perry Mason* newspaper strip in 1952, when he was just twenty-two. "Alex Raymond was my idol in my teen years and early twenties," he recalled much later. "Working in Alex's style pleased King Features, but bothered me. I struggled for several years to move away from the Raymond look. With the help, guidance, cajoling, and philosophizing of the great children's book illustrator Harry Devlin, I broke the Raymond habit. I'm still trying to find my own style." The search for a style of his own was, despite Thorne's demurrers, a successful one, and by the 1970s he was doing some of the most original and distinctive work in comic books.

Thorne still lives in the area of New Jersey where he was born in 1930. He's married to his high school sweetheart. He's said his early years were marked "with an uninterrupted passion to perform before the masses as a magician and musician." An equal interest in drawing persuaded him to enter Art Career School in New York City. While still in school he managed to do some pulp illustrating and a little comic book work. He next sold a daily strip, with the snappy title of *The Illustrated History of Union County,* to a New Jersey newspaper. "I wrote as well as drew the series. It paid 25 bucks a piece—150 smackers a week. A king's ransom. We got married."

Next came the Erle Stanley Gardner strip and then a fifteen-year association with Dell-Western. Although his style was changing, he was still in the Raymond camp. And among his early assignments were comic book versions of *Flash Gordon* and *Jungle Jim.* In 1956 he took over the soap opera strip, *Dr. Guy Bennett.* "It's a man-killing job doing a daily and a Sunday single-handed," he's said of his six years with the good doctor, "but I was young." During his time with the strip Thorne broke away from the Raymond look. He began to draw in a more realistic way, experimented with cinematic layouts, and took more chances.

The new style was in evidence in his comic book work as well, especially in the fantasy and science fiction stories in *Twilight Zone, Boris Karloff,* and *Mighty Samson.* By the time he joined up with DC in 1968 Thorne had a fully developed style of his own. He put it to good use, even though he was usually assigned the second-string characters. His work on *Tomahawk, Korak,* and *Enemy Ace* was impressive.

The major confrontation in Thorne's life took place in the middle 1970s, when he was introduced to Red Sonja. A character taken from Robert E. Howard's Conan saga and developed into a property by Roy Thomas, Red Sonja was billed by Marvel as a "She-devil With A Sword." This red-haired barbarian lady had a profound effect on Thorne and in the midst of drawing her comic book adventures he said, "Red Sonja is as real to me as you who hold this book in your hands. . . . Call it midlife crisis. Call it Faustian. Say what you will about my madness for Sonja. There is a strange, deep inner feeling that drives me to carry her standard. I love her, deeply; that should be enough."

His fondness for the she-devil caused Thorne to turn out some of his most ambitious and detailed artwork while in her service. His ancient cities, his crowded bazaars, his wizards and warriors were all done on a scale that would've made Cecil B. De Mille envious. Thorne developed new layouts, new ways of breaking down his pages. And his Sonja was depicted in a way that was sensuous and knowing. At the height of his involvement with the character Thorne began appearing at comics conventions around the country in the guise of the Wizard. The long beard and Willie Nelson hair he'd acquired helped the illusion. With various young women as Red Sonja—among them Wendy Pini of *Elfquest* fame—he staged magic shows. The boy magician from New Jersey had become the old wizard of lost and ancient times.

Since parting company with the warrior maiden, Thorne has left conventional comics. He draws pretty-girl strips for *National Lampoon* and *Playboy.* He is presently busy with a barbarian of his own creation: Ghita of Alizarr, who's thus far appeared in two black-and-white graphic novels. Tougher, and hornier, than Sonja, her impressively drawn adventures are for mature audiences only.

Red Sonja journeys through a busy Thorne landscape.

Alex Toth

One of the real mavericks of comics, Toth has been in the business for forty years and has yet to settle into a rut. His next job won't be exactly like the last one, and you can be certain he won't be drawing next year the way he was last year. He considers himself to be still learning and believes that the most important ability an artist can develop is "the ability to tell the story." Toth's restlessness, his need to push into new areas and try new ways of telling his stories, coupled with his willingness to speak up for his views, have kept him from settling into a comfortable niche. This has meant that the majority of comics fans, who tend to favor year-in–year-out consistency in their cartoonists, have been more perplexed than enthusiastic about his work. In the introduction to a Toth interview published in *Graphic Story Magazine* in 1970, Gil Kane implied that Toth—"one of the finest artists comics ever produced"—was not for the average reader and was basically an artist's artist. Fifteen years later *The Comics Journal* reprinted the interview under the title *Still The "Artist's Artist."* This may be the tag that'll stick to Toth for the rest of his career.

Alexander Toth was born in New York City in 1928. An only child, he found himself with a lot of time to fill. "I began to doodle at age three, but couldn't sell a thing until I was fifteen." He attended the High School of Industrial Arts, where he rubbed shoulders with other would-be cartoonists. While still in high school he started getting assignments from Steve Douglas at Famous Funnies, Inc. This consisted of two- and three-page stories and spot illustrations for text fillers in *Heroic Comics.* In 1947, after "pestering" him for several years, Toth was hired by Sheldon Mayer to work for the All-American division of DC. "He was terrific," Toth has said of his editor. "Warm, wildly funny, unpredictable from moment to moment, and with a great flair for dramatic impact and zany antics."

The superheroes were still thriving in those early postwar years. Toth illustrated the adventures of quite a few of them, including Green Lantern, Dr. Mid-nite, and the Atom. By this time he'd fallen under the spell of the newspaper strip work of Milton Caniff, Frank Robbins, and Noel Sickles, his lifelong idol. "What I gained from Noel," he's said, "was an appreciation for economy, clarity, line, mass, pattern, perspective, dramatic moment, subtlety, light source and drop shadow mechanics, negative and positive silhouette values, shapes and the overlapping of same, tension." Toth's stuff in this period is very good, but he still looks like a gifted disciple of the Caniff school. He hadn't yet assimilated all that Sickles had to teach. His work stood out, though, and he was soon a star at DC.

Toth moved around a good deal in the 1950s, changing his style several times. He likes to quote some advice Roy Crane once gave him—"Don't draw too much into each panel. Throw out everything you don't need to tell the story!" He did some exceptional work for an issue of *Crime and Punishment,* using doubletone paper to get his depth effects. He drew romance comics for several publishers, developing a fresh, cinematic approach that other artists went on imitating for years. He ghosted the *Casey Ruggles* newspaper strip, spent some time in the service, and then settled in Southern California. From the middle 1950s into the 1960s he did most of his comic book work for Dell-Western. Toth's specialty was comic book adaptations of movies and television shows—*Zorro, 77 Sunset Strip, Rio Bravo, Sea Hunt, The FBI Story, The Real McCoys,* etc. He was constantly experimenting, even with the basic tools he used. He was one of the first in comics to use a Rapidograph pen and the now fairly common markers.

Living in Southern California, Toth became interested in animation. He did his first work in the field in 1964 and has been in and out of it ever since, mostly as a character design man for outfits like Hanna-Barbera. He still works in comic books now and then. He did some excellent artwork for the Warren black-and-whites. His major job there was *Bravo For Adventure* in *The Rook,* which allowed him to indulge his fondness for the 1930s, airplanes, and the movies. It's no coincidence that Jesse Bravo, the daredevil stunt flyer, looks an awful lot like Errol Flynn. Toth has also worked for European publishers, on features like *Torpedo 1936.* Toward the end of that 1970 interview he admitted, "I expected to have done a lot more with it than I have. I am my biggest disappointment." It's that disappointment, of course, that keeps him going and keeps him always several lengths ahead of the pack.

YOU'RE ROLLING IN! YOUR MISSION IS FINISHED AND YOU'RE ROLLING IN! YOU STREAK ACROSS THE FIELD AT 1000 FEET IN RIGHT ECHELON! THEN...

THEN YOU GRACEFULLY PEEL OFF... BRAKE, FLAPS AND TRICYCLE LANDING GEAR DOWN, AND YOUR SKIMMING MACHINE *TOUCHES GROUND AGAIN!*

YOU HAVE LANDED! YOU NOW TAXI YOUR JET DOWN TO THE GROUP OF WAITING CREWMEN! NEWS OF YOUR VICTORY HAS ALREADY REACHED THEM!

YOU SHOVE BACK THE CANOPY, JERK OFF THE CLUMSY HELMET AND YOU CLIMB TO THE GROUND TO INSPECT DAMAGE THE MIGS HAVE DONE TO YOUR STURDY PLANE!

AND AS YOU FINGER THE TORN ALUMINUM, YOU THINK OF THE 20 MM CANNON THE MIGS HAVE!

AND THEN YOU THINK HOW THE MIGS GO FASTER THAN YOU, AND YOU THINK HOW THE MIGS OUTNUMBER YOU...

AND YOU THINK OF THAT CLASSROOM IN THE SKY! AND THEN YOU THINK...WE'D BETTER DO SOMETHING, *SOON...*

...PRETTY GOL-DARNED SOON!

A forceful and cinematic page, putting to use everything he'd learned from the work of artists like Noel Sickles. *(Copyright © 1986 William M. Gaines.)*

George Tuska

A veteran of nearly a half-century in comic books, Tuska has worked for just about every major publisher and quite a few minor ones. He's drawn superheroes, cowboys, jungle girls, gangbusters, clowns, and magicians. In his spare time he's turned out the newspaper strip adventures of Scorchy Smith, Buck Rogers, and Superman.

Tuska started out in the shops, working first for Eisner-Iger and then for Chesler. His earliest published work showed up in *Mystery Men Comics, Speed Comics,* and *Wonderworld Comics.* Already Tuska was developing, in the features he drew for these magazines, two of his lifelong graphic specialties—pretty women and boats. He branched out considerably in the early 1940s. For Fawcett he produced the second and third issues of the newly launched *Captain Marvel Adventures,* and also did Golden Arrow in *Whiz* and El Carim in *Master.* The latter fellow was but one of the several magicians he worked on at the time; Zanzibar and Hale the Magician were others.

At Quality he depicted several characters, most notably Uncle Sam in that superpatriot's own short-lived magazine. Tuska was, as alluded to earlier, a pioneering practitioner of what's come to be called Good Girl Art. The chief Golden Age manufacturer of this product was T. T. Scott's Fiction House and Tuska served six years with the outfit. He drew attractive ladies in a variety of occupations, from jungle goddess to airplane pilot. Among them were Camilla in *Jungle Comics,* Glory Forbes in *Rangers,* and Jane Martin in *Wings.* He also drew a definite second-banana superguy, the Hooded Wasp, for *Shadow Comics* and even managed some humor fillers for Marvel's earliest comedy titles.

The Tuska style at this period blended illustrational and cartoon elements. It was lean and uncluttered, especially effective with fantasy and comedy. Tuska was always a good figure man and his layouts were strong. By the middle of the 1940s, his work had become much more realistic, partly because he was hired to work on *Crime Does Not Pay.* There he illustrated more or less true stories that were packed with hoodlums, killers, gun molls, fast cars, and tommy-guns. He soon took over the lead-off yarn, the one narrated by Mr. Crime, who was a cross between radio's sardonic Whistler and Mr. Coffee Nerves from the Postum newspaper comic section ads. A good deal of violence and bloodshed showed up in the comic books in the immediate postwar years, and this *Crime Does Not Pay* stuff shows Tuska in his most gritty and hard-boiled phase.

During these same years he did a great deal of drawing for books such as *Exciting* and *Thrilling,* working on surviving superheroes like the Black Terror and the original Doc Strange. He returned to Marvel in the 1950s, turning out material for Western, war, romance, and crime titles. The rebirth of the superhero genre in the 1960s led to his serving time with the Avengers, X-Men, Ka-Zar, Daredevil, the Hulk, Sub-Mariner, Luke Cage, and Captain America. For the Tower line he contributed to the Thunder Agents saga.

The 1970s found him working on *Challengers of the Unknown, Superman,* and *Legion of Superheroes* at DC. He also pencilled the *World's Greatest Super-Heroes* newspaper strip, launched by DC to take advantage of the popularity of the Superman movies.

The super-gang strip was Tuska's third newspaper venture. From 1954 to 1959 he both drew and wrote *Scorchy Smith* for the Associated Press. This was the aviation strip begun in 1930 and worked on by such exceptional artists as Noel Sickles, Bert Christman, and Frank Robbins. Tuska graduated from *Scorchy* to the best-known science fiction hero in the world. He drew *Buck Rogers* until its demise in 1967.

Over the years his work has become less vital, less interesting. A very prolific penciller, he has been too often at the mercy of inkers less talented than he. To see Tuska at his best you have to look back to the forties.

From a story done while Tuska was the king of crime. *(Copyright © 1948 Lev Gleason Publications, Inc.)*

Ed Wheelan

He typified one of the major groups that worked in comic books during the first big boom of the late 1930s and early 1940s—the years when, to meet the continually increasing demand for new material, artists were recruited from all over. Some were kids fresh out of school, some were veteran illustrators from the pulp magazines, and some were former newspaper strip cartoonists. Wheelan belonged to this last category, which included such diverse talents as George Storm, Bert Christman, Tom McNamara, Paul Fung, and C. A. Voight.

He worked in comic books from the late thirties through the early fifties. Irreverent when it came to the more serious conventions of popular culture, he spent those years kidding movies, radio, and even the supermen who helped pay his salary. He also found time to concoct a highly entertaining burlesque of Sherlock Holmes in comic book form, purvey hundreds of the most bewhiskered old vaudeville jokes and, singlehanded, produce one of the earliest EC titles. And all this, Wheelan felt certain, was after his real career had ended.

Edgar Stow Wheelan was born in 1888, and by the time World War I started he was well established as a newspaper cartoonist. In the early 1920s, after having done various strips for the Hearst newspapers, he created *Minute Movies,* which became one of the most successful features of the decade. Gradually Wheelan introduced a regular cast of characters. These included blond, handsome Dick Dare, blonde, pretty Hazel Dearie, villainous Ralph McSneer, and others. Using the motion pictures of the day as a take-off point, Wheelan put his cast thorough every kind of format: cowboy continuities, airplane adventures, soldier of fortune yarns, detective stories, and comedies. He also kidded newsreels, travelogues, and just about everything else you were likely to encounter in a movie palace. As newspaper strips grew more serious in the Depression years, Wheelan started doing longer stories and also adapting such classics as *Ivanhoe* and *Hamlet.* The strip folded in the middle 1930s.

One of Wheelan's lifelong fascinations was with the circus, and his last strip, done in the mid-thirties, was *Big Top.* This didn't succeed and Wheelan, who long believed that William Randolph Hearst had a hand in his career troubles, went out of business as a comic strip artist. For quite a while, he kept hoping for a comeback, but that never happened. What happened instead was comic books.

The first Wheelan work to appear in comic books was reprints of his *Big Top* stuff in *Feature Funnies.* In the summer and fall of 1938 the Centaur company put out two issues of *Little Giant Movie Funnies.* Copy inside these small six-and-one-half- by four-and-one-half-inch black-and-white-magazines touted the fact they were providing a "whole motion picture show for a dime!!!" No mention was made that the contents reprinted *Minute Movies* newspaper strips.

Late in 1939 *Flash Comics* was launched. In addition to the Flash himself, you got Hawkman, the Whip, and Johnny Thunder. And editor Sheldon Mayer had hired Wheelan to do an eight page-feature. Wheelan's first original material for comic books was called *Flash Picture Novels* and was quite close to *Minute Movies.* In *Flash* #12 (December, 1940), Wheelan gave in to "popular demand" and brought back *Minute Movies.* He drew forty-three new installments in all. As he'd done with the newspaper strip, he alternated melodramas and burlesques. Along with the movies ran animated cartoons, comedy shorts, and travelogues.

On the comedy page two of the MM actors, Fuller Phun and Archibald Clubb, teamed up as Fat and Slat. They proved quite popular, and the first complete Fat-and-Slat comic book was issued in 1944. It was a compendium of one-pagers in which the team did its best to perpetrate some of the most venerable and god-awful jokes known to man. When M. C. Gaines ended his association with DC to start his EC line, he hired Wheelan to do a Fat-and-Slat quarterly. This lasted four issues, from 1947 to 1948, and offered yet more ancient jokes and gags.

Another major Wheelan achievement of the forties was *The Adventures of Padlock Homes.* Done for the Harvey Brothers, it began in *Champ Comics* in the spring of 1942 and then moved over to *Speed Comics* in 1943. More than a burlesque of Sir Arthur Conan Doyle's celebrated sleuth, it was also a parody of detective melodramas in general, movie serials, and anything else that caught Wheelan's fancy.

Throughout his comic book career, Wheelan used the style he'd perfected in the 1920s. It was lively, scratchy, and unashamedly bigfoot and did much to add variety to the comic books of the 1940s. By the early 1950s he was out of the field. When he died in Florida in 1966, he was working on, appropriately enough, a series of clown paintings.

The quintessence of the bigfoot style. *(Copyright © 1986 William M. Gaines.)*

Al Williamson

The impact of Alex Raymond on comic book art was considerable. His *Flash Gordon* Sunday pages were first reprinted in *King Comics* early in 1936, and by the late 1930s and early 1940s disciples such as John Lehti, George Papp, and Sheldon Moldoff were doing original comic book work in their own versions of Raymond's heroic dry-brush style. Al Williamson, perhaps the most successful Raymond idolator of them all, started working in comics in 1948. Eventually he got a chance to draw several Raymond creations, including *Flash Gordon* and *Secret Agent X-9*.

Williamson was born in New York in 1931 and grew up in Bogotá, Colombia. His first encounter with *Flash Gordon* was in Spanish-language reprints. He and his family returned to the United States in the early 1940s and while in his teens he began attending the New York Cartoonists & Illustrators School. His teacher for the Saturday-morning sketch class was Burne Hogarth. It was Hogarth's practice to have his more gifted pupils help out on *Tarzan,* and Williamson took a turn pencilling some Sunday pages in 1948.

Over at Famous Funnies, Inc., the page rates weren't high, and editor Steve Douglas was receptive to young artists. For Douglas's *Heroic Comics* #51 (November, 1948) Williamson did his first professional comic book work, a two-page story entitled *Thin Ice on Shell Bank Creek,* about an incident of everyday heroism. He soon moved on to Westerns and by 1950, with some inking help from his friend Frank Frazetta, Williamson was doing the lead stories in Toby Press's *John Wayne.* He also drew for the company's *Billy The Kid,* most notably a story based on the exploits of movie hero Rock Hudson.

By the following year Williamson was able to indulge his interest in fantasy and science fiction. He started doing work, sometimes assisted by Roy Krenkel and sometimes by Frazetta, for *Forbidden Worlds, Danger Is Our Business, Jet,* and *Out of the Night.* In 1952, just before he turned twenty-one, he commenced his association with EC. He went up there at the suggestion of Wally Wood and was hired. He's said that that period was an enjoyable one for him. "A lot of guys were already married and had to turn the stuff out and make a living and pay the bills," he's explained, "but I was kind of footloose and fancy-free. So it didn't bother me too much. I could play the prima donna and get away with it."

Williamson did some of his best-remembered artwork during the four years he was with EC. Most of his output appeared in *Weird Fantasy* and *Weird Science,* and later in tamer EC titles like *Valor* and *Piracy.* It was here that he fully developed his sweeping panoramas, intricate jungle landscapes, and towering fantasy cities. Williamson continued to rely on his various artist buddies for assistance. He explained his reasons for this by saying, "Well, Frank and Roy and Angelo Torres were all good friends. And I enjoyed drawing figures very much. I didn't like drawing backgrounds. And I was deathly afraid of the brush—I was afraid I'd botch up the inking with the brush. . . . Frank, I think, inked roughly about two or three jobs for me, and I pencilled them. Roy Krenkel pencilled the backgrounds and I inked those. But one of the main reasons, I guess, that I worked with them was that we had a hell of a lot of fun."

After EC, Williamson drew for a number of other publishers, including Marvel, where he did horror, Western, romance, and war stories. Finally in the middle 1960s he got to draw *Flash Gordon* for King Features's short-lived line of comic books. He also did a *Secret Agent X-9* short story. Williamson says he told King, "I want the filler to be *X-9* so I have this break of doing a civilian thing, because I hate doing the same thing all the time." Soon after that the syndicate offered him the *X-9* newspaper strip. He began drawing it in 1967, under the new title of *Secret Agent Corrigan,* with Archie Goodwin providing the scripts. He stayed with the spy strip until 1980.

Williamson next did an adaptation of *The Empire Strikes Back* for Marvel and an adaptation of the *Flash Gordon* movie for Western. Williamson, with Goodwin doing the writing, took over the *Star Wars* comic strip and stayed with it until it folded. He feels that "the papers don't seem to want adventure strips . . . they just want funny stuff." Presently he is working again in comic books and will probably stay there for awhile. "Well, I've got to keep making money," he explains. "I've got a family to feed."

A Williamson specialty, flamboyant science-fantasy. *(Copyright © 1974 Marvel Comics Group.)*

Barry Windsor-Smith

It was with the help of a barbarian that Smith first gained recognition and attention; namely, the most famous barbarian of them all—Conan. The London-born Smith was just twenty-one when he became, in 1970, the first artist to draw Marvel's *Conan the Barbarian.* That same year his peers in the Academy of Comic Book Arts voted him best new talent. In both 1971 and 1972 *Conan* was judged the best comic book by the ACBA, and in 1972 Smith was also named best artist by the fans. Nothing he's done since has quite equalled the impact of that early work in the realm of swords and sorcery.

Smith's first few issues of *Conan the Barbarian* were a bit shaky and unsure. "His strong sense of design and ability to pick precisely the right angles set him apart, though," as one critic has pointed out, "and each book he drew was better than the last." It probably stands to reason that an artist who lists his two major influences as Jack Kirby and Alphonse Mucha would turn out pages that were somewhat different from the usual Marvel bullpen product. As Smith developed and improved, his renderings of these tales of the Hyborean Age displayed an appealing blend of comic book and art nouveau touches. Smith's material, notes *The World Encyclopedia of Comics,* "was heavily-laden with intricate designs—at times bordering on ornate, art deco-like scenes and backgrounds—and eye-pleasing composition and layout." By the time he gave up drawing Robert E. Howard's warrior king, his work had matured even further and he'd assimilated even more. These later pages are impressively done and are among the few in comics that have a strong pre-Raphaelite look. Because of the wide range of his influences Smith brought a new look to the comics of the seventies. Since then several lesser artists have been influenced by him.

Smith left the *Conan* color comic after issue #24, having stayed around long enough to introduce Red Sonja. He also drew Conan for the early issues of the black-and-white *Savage Tales,* which debuted in 1971 and offered somewhat more adult material. Smith did a few jobs as well for *Savage Sword of Conan,* a black-and-white magazine that came along in 1974. He also worked on a handful of other features for Marvel, drawing, briefly, *Daredevil, Iron Man, Tower of Shadows,* and *Dr. Strange.* "If Smith was perfect for conjuring up Conan's era," one comics historian has commented, "he was just as clever at inventing a mysterious world for Strange's tales of the constant struggle between white and black magic. Like Steve Ditko and Gene Colan before him, Smith rose to the task of interpreting Strange and his version ranks with the best." In addition, Smith contributed drawings to magazines ranging from *New York* to *National Lampoon.*

Smith pretty much took a leave of absence from comic books in the middle 1970s. He founded Gorblimey Press to produce his own posters and portfolios and has made infrequent returns to comics, turning out stories for *Star Reach* and *Epic Illustrated.* More recently he's worked on a *Machine Man* miniseries and drawn three issues of *X-Men* and a *Thing* story for *Marvel Fanfare.*

A beautifully rendered Conan page, as our hero battles a tentacled horror while complaining about the opposite sex. Script by Roy Thomas. *(Copyright © 1974 Marvel Comics Group.)*

Basil Wolverton

He billed himself as a producer of preposterous pictures of the peculiar people who prowl this perplexing planet, and from the late 1930s into the early 1950s Wolverton turned out some of the most audacious and individual humor pages to be found in comic books. He also drew some of the most wildly adventurous science fiction ever seen in comic books. He could only have flourished in the eclectic comic book business of forty years ago, when nobody was quite certain what you could and couldn't get away with.

His magnum opus in the funny field was undoubtedly Powerhouse Pepper. It was for Marvel that he created the character, the only bald-headed superhero of his day, in the spring of 1942. Powerhouse, who first showed up in *Joker Comics* #1, didn't own a superman suit and usually combatted evil wearing a striped turtleneck sweater, slacks, and heavy workshoes. The feature was very much in tune with the sort of baggy-pants burlesque comedy that was popular during World War II. Before Powerhouse was many issues old, Wolverton had given way to his compulsive fascination with alliteration and eventually he reached a point where he couldn't even sign his name straight. Instead he'd use "by Basil Baboonbrain Wolverton," "by Basil Weirdwit Wolverton," "by Basil Bucketbeak Wolverton," etc. He was equally fond of internal rhyme, and his dialogue as well as the numerous signs and posters that cluttered almost every inch of wall—and often the floor and ceiling as well—were full of the stuff. "Zounds! Your snappers are as sound as a hound's," observes one of the physicians giving Powerhouse his army physical. The three doctors are Dr. Ash Gash, Dr. Bill Drill, and Dr. Jack Hack.

All in all Wolverton produced nearly five hundred pages about Powerhouse over the next seven years, sending him to just about every spot on Earth and to some heretofore unknown planets. His hairless hero held forth in *Joker, Gay Comics, Tessie the Typist, Millie the Model,* and in five issues of his own magazine. For some reason there was a five-year lapse between issue #1 and issue #2. "I was never able to make much sense of their publishing policies," Wolverton once recalled. "To even matters, though, they were never able to make much sense out of what they bought from me."

Before the forties concluded he turned out over three hundred pages of other funny stuff for comic books. His humor features included Flap Flipflop the Flying Flash, Mystic Moot and his Magic Snoot (a parody of Ibis the Invincible that appeared in the magician's own magazine), Bingbang Buster and His Horse Hedy, the Culture Corner (conducted by Dr. Croucher K. Cronk, Q.O.C., short for Queer Old Coot), and Scoop Scuttle. Scoop, a reporter on the *Daily Dally,* almost made it into the world of newspaper strips. In 1944 United Features signed Wolverton up and offered a *Scoop Scuttle* daily strip. According to Wolverton nothing came of this because "there was a newsprint cutback because of the war . . . Scoop was scuttled."

Unlike many of his comic book contemporaries, Wolverton didn't work in the Manhattan area. A native of the Pacific Northwest, he stayed out there most of the time and did his contributing by mail. After breaking into comic books in the late thirties he also tried his hand at science fiction. His major work in this vein was *Spacehawk,* which began in *Target Comics* in 1940. In this feature he depicted the intricate alien landscapes that came to characterize his highly individual version of the universe. The decor of most of his planets, moons, and asteroids was dominated by monolithic piles of rock, deep jagged chasms, and warty foliage suggestive of elephantine vegetables, gigantic innards, and runaway fungi. The extraterrestrial races he peopled his awesome planets with were usually a mixture of the vegetable and the phallic, most often resembling mobile cucumbers and gherkins.

Much of the stuff Wolverton did after leaving comic books is not his best. He upped the ugly content, drawing people who looked even more like private parts, animated intestines, or malignant growths. This is especially notable in his book *Barflize* and in what he drew for *Mad* and *Plop.* In his later years he also did some serious illustrations based on the Bible for a religious magazine called *The Plain Truth.* He died in the early 1980s.

In one of his last interviews he listed his biblical drawings as his favorite work of his entire career. But when asked what he'd like to be remembered for, Wolverton replied, "Some people will remember me longest for the disreputable pants I wear around home. . . . Regarding comic books, I should like to be remembered for *Powerhouse Pepper.*"

Spacehawk featured Wolverton's bizarre vegetation and alien creatures. *(Copyright © 1940 Novelty Press, Inc.)*

Wally Wood

Wood was one of the bright young men who burned out too soon, the comics field equivalent of jazz musicians like Bix Beiderbecke and Charlie Parker. He was an impressive artist, was successful while still youthful, and then proceeded, self-jinxed, to betray his talent and destroy himself.

A kid from Minnesota and mostly self-taught, Wood began drawing for comic books when he was twenty. In 1949, still in his early twenties, he went to work for EC. "After being exploited by nearly everyone in the business," he once explained, "I finally found a home at good old EC." In talking about Wood's work during this period, Pete Hamill has said, "The drawing was wonderful. Wood had learned much from the men who came before him; his faces owed a debt to Hal Foster . . . Wood's women were derived from Eisner, as were his deep rich shadings and the dazzling patterns of his comic book pages. But Wood had taken these influences, mixed them up, and made something of his own."

He worked on all the EC titles, but it was in the science fiction books—*Weird Science* and *Weird Fantasy*—that he excelled. He developed a way of drawing gadgets, technical hardware, space gear, and spacecraft that was distinctly his own. Many a later artist borrowed from him. The impressive Wood clutter became a trademark. In a story called *My World* in *Weird Science,* he appeared as himself in the final panel to explain his credo directly to the reader. "My world is the world of science-fiction," he explained. "Conceived in my mind and placed upon paper with pencil and ink and brush and sweat and a great deal of love for my world. For I am a science-fiction artist. My name is Wood."

For *Mad* he worked in a lighter manner, one that sometimes hinted at Walt Kelly as a source of inspiration. He stayed with the magazine when it switched from comic book to black-and-white format and also drew for many of its imitators—*Panic, Humbug, Trump,* and *Plop.* Wood had a knack for imitating and kidding the work of others and this served him well in doing takeoffs of Caniff, Disney, and *Peanuts.*

Wood accomplished quite a bit in the 1950s. He served a stint of ghosting *The Spirit,* collaborated with Jack Kirby on an unsuccessful SF newspaper strip called *Sky Masters,* and did illustrations for *Galaxy* and other science fiction magazines and comic book work for Marvel, Harvey, Charlton, and DC. He also began turning out advertising art for such accounts as Alka-Seltzer and Dr. Pepper, as well as gum cards for Topps.

Although his work in the 1960s wasn't as strong, he was kept busy. For Marvel he worked on such superheroes as the Avengers, Daredevil, and the Human Torch. The Tower line hired him to create and sometimes draw *T.H.U.N.D.E.R. Agents.* He even drew for semiunderground publications like *The Realist.* The Disney parody he did for the latter publication showed a crude, nasty side of Wood that was, unfortunately, to surface more and more as time went by.

Wood's lifestyle and method of working weren't exactly conducive to good health and well-being. There were periods of heavy drinking, alternating with back-breaking stretches of drawing. Overworked, sometimes running a free-form sort of sweatshop to get the stuff out, Wood plugged ahead. Increasingly unhappy with most of his editors, he decided to become a publisher himself. This resulted in an initially impressive magazine he called *witzend.* In another of his publications he took several swings at editors. "Do not seek to be a creative writer or artist," he advised. "Do not CARE about doing anything good. That will only put you at the mercy of those who will always hate you because you can do something they can't."

In the 1970s, he did some less than first-rate inking for DC and others. For military-oriented publications he drew *Cannon,* a hard-boiled intrigue feature, and *Sally Forth,* a comedy-adventure strip in the *Annie Fanny* mode. He returned to fantasy late in the decade, doing an impressive job on *The Wizard King.* In 1978 Wood had a stroke. "I saw some of the late drawings and they were heartbreaking," Hammil said. "Wood's art had always been marked by a fluid accuracy; he could draw immense spaceships in precise detail, and make a human face laugh with a few lines. Looking at those late drawings, you knew something was terribly wrong." In his last years Wood also suffered from kidney disease. Among the last things he drew were some pathetic stories for a pornographic comic book.

By 1981 his health had deteriorated even further. In November of that year Wood shot himself.

Earlier, reflecting on his career, he had said, "I don't worry about words, like whether I'm an illustrator or a cartoonist or whatever. I'm an artist; I do it for a living. . . . Looking back, I had fun. For the first five years of EC I was having a ball. I would rather draw than eat maybe."

It's a personal feeling, this... not scientific, not cold and clear, but deeply personal...

The Wood approach to gadgetry, in the service of the Spirit. *(Copyright © 1986 Will Eisner.)*

Berni Wrightson

Like several younger generation comic book artists, Wrightson has built his style out of bits and pieces of the styles of earlier comic book artists. "I think any other artist I ever looked at I studied to one extent or another, and learned something from," he replied when asked about his influences. "It's hard to say where anything comes from. It's all this big hodgepodge. And it's hopefully something original by the time I'm done with it." Narrowing down the list to a handful of people, he said his major sources of inspiration had been "most of the EC guys and Frazetta." That he's successfully assimilated all his influences—including Al Williamson, Graham Ingels, and Frank Frazetta—is evidenced by the enthusiastic acceptance his work has met with. *The Comics Journal* has called him "possibly the most popular artist to emerge from comics' short-lived renaissance of the late 1960s."

Bernard Albert Wrightson was born in 1948 and began working in comic books in 1969. By that time he'd already appeared in assorted fanzines and worked as a staff cartoonist on the Baltimore *Sun.* Of this latter job he's said, "I just worked in a big room with a bunch of other artists and most of the work was photo retouching and paste-up, layout-type work and not a lot of cartooning or illustrating."

Wrightson drew *Nightmaster* for DC and then began illustrating stories for their *House of Mystery* and *House of Secrets.* By this time, the early 1970s, both these titles were doing sedate versions of the EC horror tales of twenty years before, complete with grotesque hosts and heavily ironic endings. Wrightson, who'd grown up on ECs, fit right in. He also concocted quite a few intricate yet poster-like covers. During this period Wrightson, in collaboration with writer Len Wein, created what has been called "his greatest popular success in comics." Swamp Thing first lurched into view in

House of Secrets #92 (June–July, 1971). By autumn of the following year he had his own bimonthly. Wrightson did some imaginative work with the character, paying homage not only to EC but to dozens of horror movies he'd seen and relished in his youth. The impression made by his *Swamp Thing* was chiefly responsible for his winning the best artist award from the now-defunct Academy of Comic Book Arts two years in a row. He abandoned the character in 1974 to move over to Warren.

At Warren—in *Creepy, Eerie,* and *Vampirella*—Wrightson worked in black and white. He has a knack for getting strong effects with light and shadow, which he used well in these stories. There were adaptations of H. P. Lovecraft and Poe as well as some written by Wrightson himself. By this time he'd discovered illustrators like Joseph Clement Coll and Franklin Booth and was applying some of their techniques. Booth (1874–1948) had adapted the look of steel and wood engravings to pen-and-ink drawings, an approach Wrightson utilized on several of his Warren tales.

He's also done full-color posters and tried his hand at portfolios. Among them was one based on Edgar Allan Poe stories and another derived from *Frankenstein.* In 1982 he did a comic book adaptation of the George Romero-Stephen King movie *Creepshow.* A long-time admirer of King's books, he recently illustrated King's *Cycle of the Werewolf.* "I've read everything he's ever written. Yeah, I'm a big fan of his."

Wrightson is likely to keep experimenting and branching out. He has in the past dropped out of comics, saying things like, "I've reached a point where I've outgrown comics." More recently he's retracted such statements, explaining, "I realize now that I never did and probably never will." Yet he still feels it's important to get away from the field periodically.

The chilling, atmospheric world of Berni Wrightson. *(Copyright © 1984 Berni Wright-son.)*

The Great Comic Book Artists
An Informal Bibliography

What follows is a suggested reading/looking/collecting list. It's selective and by no means complete, giving just the highlights of each artist's career and what we consider the best examples of his work. Along with original comic book appearances, we've also included some reprints and compilations. Most of these are easier to come by and a good deal less expensive.

For those of you who want fuller listings, we suggest consulting Robert Overstreet's *Comic Book Price Guide* and Jerry Bails's *Who's Who of American Comic Books*. Overstreet also provides dates and current prices for most of the titles on our list.

Neal Adams

Deadman 1–7 (1985 reprints)

Echo of Futurepast 1–4

Green Lantern 76–87, 89

Green Lantern/Green Arrow 1–7 (1983 reprints)

X-Men 56–63

X-Men Classics 1–3 (1983 reprints)

Matt Baker

Classics Illustrated 32

Fight 36–60

Golden Features 1 (Blackthorne, 1985)
   Reprints Baker's *Flamingo* strip.

Phantom Lady 13–23

Carl Barks

Barks Bear Book
   Reprints 32 of his non-duck stories.

The most accessible source of Barks's Disney material is Another Rainbow Publishing, Inc. Their Carl Barks Library series and their Gladstone line of comic books contain reprints of much of Barks's Donald Duck and Uncle Scrooge material.

Dan Barry

Action 131–185

Gangbusters 1–10

C. C. Beck

Fatman 1–3

Shazam! 1–10

Whiz 1–22

Charles Biro

Boy 3 to date
   Biro did covers for this title long after he stopped drawing any stories.

Crime Does Not Pay
   Covers for several years.

Daredevil 2–10 (first series, 1941)
   Plus many covers on later issues.

Zip 1–15

Dick Briefer

Frankenstein 1–33

Prize 7–54, 56–68

John Buscema

Avengers 41–66

Conan 25–36, 41–56, 93–126

Savage Sword of Conan 1–5, 47–58

John Byrne

Alpha Flight 1–28

E-Man 6–9

Fantastic Four 209–218, 251–267, 269 to date

Incredible Hulk 314 to date

Marvel Preview 11

X-Men 108–109, 111–143

At one time or another, Byrne has also drawn virtually every character at Marvel.

George Carlson

Jingle Jangle 1–42

Puzzle Fun Comics 1–2

With the exception of some puzzle pages in *Famous Funnies,* the above represents Carlson's complete contribution to comic books.

Howard Chaykin

American Flagg! 1–12, 15–26

Star Wars 1–10

Gene Colan

Howard the Duck (comic) 4–15, 17–20, 24–27, 30–31

Nathaniel Dusk 1–4

Nathaniel Dusk 2 1–4

Night Force 1–14

Tomb of Dracula 1–70

Jack Cole

National 13

Police Comics 1–30
   Ghost artists and a less dedicated Cole are in evidence in later issues

Smash 18–38

Reed Crandall

Blackhawk 10–11
Feature 44–60
Military 12–22

Crandall's EC work can most easily be seen by way of Russ Cochran's various albums and reprints.

Jack Davis

Rawhide Kid 33–35, 125
Yak Yak 1–2 (Dell 4-Color 1186, 1348)

The Cochran books and magazines are also the best source of Davis's EC work.

Steve Ditko

Amazing Spider-Man 1–38, Annual 1–2 (reprinted in *Marvel Tales* 137–177)
Captain Atom 78–87
Blue Beetle 1–5 (1967)
Tales of the Mysterious Traveler 2–12

Will Eisner

National 1–3
Smash 1–13
Will Eisner's Quarterly 1 to date

The most economical source of *The Spirit* is the series of reprint books and magazines issued by Kitchen Sink Press, Inc.

Lee Elias

Adventure 257–269
Black Cat 3–29
Rangers 21–28
Rook 1–7

George Evans

Blackhawk 244–246
Captain Video 1–6

Evans's EC work is available in the Cochran reprints.

Bill Everett

Daredevil 1 (first series, 1941)
Heroic 1–9, 12

Marvel Mystery 1–28
Menace 1–6

Lou Fine

Crack 1–4, 11–22
National 12–18
Smash 14–22
Wonderworld 3–11

Fine also produced many covers for *Hit, National, Wonderworld,* and *Mystery Men.*

Frank Frazetta

Durango Kid 1–16
Shining Knight 1, 2
Thun'da 1
White Indian 11

Fred Guardineer

Action 1–28
Big Shot 1–14
Durango Kid 19–41

Paul Gustavson

Marvel Mystery 1–21
Police 1–22
Smash 22–67

Bob Kane

Famous 1st Edition F-6
    Reprints *Batman* 1.
Famous First Edition C-28
    Reprints *Detective* 27.

Gil Kane

Conan the Barbarian 127–134
Green Lantern 1–61, 68–75, 156
Sword of the Atom 1–4, Special 1–2

Walt Kelly

Pogo Possum 1–16
Fairy Tale Parade 1–9
Our Gang 1–6, 8, 10–58

Plans are afoot to reprint all of Kelly's comic book work.

Jack Kirby

Adventure 72–90
Detective Comics 64–83
Fantastic Four 1–102
New Gods 1–6 (1984 reprints)
Journey into Mystery 83–90, 101–125

This is, perhaps, a good place to remind you that our lists are not complete and provide only highlights. Kirby's full bibliography, after nearly a half century in comic books, would fill this entire section and then some.

Bernard Krigstein

Journey into Unknown Worlds 11, 12, 43
Marvel Tales 98, 106–107, 142, 157, 159
Strange Tales 10, 15, 22, 42, 45, 59, 61

Yet again the Cochran reprints are the best source of Krigstein's EC work.

Joe Kubert

The Brave and the Bold 1–24
Flash Comics 62–76, 88–104
Our Army at War 83–170

Harvey Kurtzman

Harvey Kurtzman Comics
Goodman Beaver

Kurtzman's EC work is available in the Cochran reprints.

Joe Maneely

Black Knight 1–5
Red Dragon 5–7 (second series)
Ringo Kid 1, 4, 5
Speed Carter, Spaceman 1–7

Jesse Marsh

Tarzan 1–153
Gene Autry 1–25
John Carter of Mars 1–3 (Gold Key reprints, 1964)

Sheldon Mayer

All-American 1–59
Best of DC 29, 37, 41, 43, 47, 55
Funny Stuff 5
  SM wrote and drew the entire issue, including cover.
Sugar & Spike 1–98

Mort Meskin

Action 42–121 (most issues)
Golden Lad 1–5
Shield Wizard 3, 4
Top-Notch 2–8

Frank Miller

Daredevil 158–191 (1979–1983)
Marvel Team-Up 100
Ronin 1–6

Bob Montana

Archie 1
Jackpot 4, 5
Pep 22–36

Klaus Nordling

Lady Luck 86–90
National 1–22, 42–72
Smash 42–85

Nordling's *Lady Luck* is also available in two Ken Pierce trade paperbacks. His *Pen Miller* can be found in the recent Blackthorne reprint of the first issue of *National Comics*.

George Pérez

Avengers 141–144, 147–162, 167–171, 194–000
Crisis on Infinite Earths 1–12
New Teen Titans/Tales of the Teen Titans (1980–1984) 1–4, 6–34, 37–50, Annual 1–3
New Teen Titans (1984–1985) 1–5

Pérez has also drawn many other strips for Marvel, and countless covers for both Marvel and DC.

Wendy Pini

Elfquest 1–21

Elfquest 1 to date (Marvel color reprints of the above material)

Bob Powell

Cave Girl 11–14

Jumbo 5–28

Man in Black 1–4

Military 1–13

Shadow Vol. 6 No. 12 – Vol. 9 No. 5

Powell's *Mr. Mystic* has been reprinted in some of Kitchen Sink's *Spirit* magazines.

Mac Raboy

Green Lama 1–8

Master Comics 15–39

Jerry Robinson

Batman 37
  Entire issue is by Robinson.

Black Terror 23–26 (with Mort Meskin)

Detective 71–73, 74–76, 79

Fighting Yank 25–29 (with Meskin)

Green Hornet 21, 25–29

John Romita

Amazing Spider-Man 39–95, 106–118

Alex Schomburg

Jon Juan 1
  One of the very few examples of his interior artwork.

Numerous issues of 1940s Marvel titles are graced with his distinctive covers. His covers are also to be found on issues of *Green Hornet, Speed, Exciting, The Black Terror,* and *The Fighting Yank.* To name but a few.

John Severin

Prize Comics Western 85–109

Severin's most impressive work can be found in the Cochran EC reprints.

Joe Shuster

Famous 1st Edition C-26
  Reprints *Action* 1.

Famous 1st Edition C-61
  Reprints *Superman* 1.

Bill Sienkiewicz

Moon Knight 1–15, 17–20, 22–26, 28–30

Moon Knight Special Edition 1–3 (1983 reprints)

New Mutants 18–31

Walt Simonson

Detective 437–443

Thor 337–354, 357 to date

John Stanley

The best source of Stanley's work is the new Little Lulu Library series published by Another Rainbow.

James Steranko

Strange Tales 151–163

Nick Fury, Agent of S.H.I.E.L.D. 1–2 (1983 reprints)

Frank Thorne

Korak, Son of Tarzan 46–51

Red Sonja 1–11

Son of Tomahawk 131–140

Alex Toth

All-American 88, 92, 96, 98–102

Adventure 418–419

Crime and Punishment 66
  Entire issue is by Toth.

Rook 3–4

George Tuska

Crime Does Not Pay 51–64

Jungle 5–13, 46–55

Uncle Sam 3

Ed Wheelan

Fat & Slat 1–4

Flash Comics 1–58

Speed Comics 25–37

Two episodes of Wheelan's *Padlock Holmes* are reprinted in Bill Blackbeard's *Sherlock Holmes in America* (Abrahams, 1979).

Al Williamson

Flash Gordon 3–5 (King, 1960s)

John Wayne 2–4, 6–8, 16, 18

Williamson's EC stuff is in the Cochran reprints.

Barry Windsor-Smith

Conan 1–16, 19–24

Conan Special Edition (1982 reprint)

Epic 16

Savage Tales 1–3

Basil Wolverton

Joker 1–27, 29–31

Target Vol. 1, No. 5 – Vol. 3, No. 10

Six adventures of Wolverton's lone wolf of space are to be found in Archival Press's 1978 *Spacehawk* trade paperback.

Wally Wood

Thunder Agents 1–11

Wood's EC work is available in the Cochran reprints. His Spirit stories are in *The Outer Space Spirit* (Kitchen Sink, 1983).

Berni Wrightson

House of Mystery 193–195, 204, 207, 209

House of Secrets 92–94, 96, 100, 103

Swamp Thing 1–10